GOLDEN HART GUIDES
BRITISH CRAFTS

GOLDEN HART GUIDES

British Crafts

Philippa Lewis

SIDGWICK & JACKSON LONDON
in association with Trusthouse Forte

Acknowledgements
The author would like to thank the
following for their help: Tessa Clegg,
glassmaker; Kathleen McFarlane, weaver;
Nan Palmer, potter and Alison Richards,
jeweller and silversmith. Also Abigail Frost
and the Crafts Council.

Contents

Photo acknowledgements
Front cover: Jewellery maker (British
Tourist Authority) Back cover: Basket
maker (British Tourist Authority)
Frontispiece: Glass engraver
(Mark Bury/photo Cambridge Evening
News); 6 Alfred Bentley; 8, 10 David Drew;
11 Peter Murphy; 12 Mary Rogers;
14 John Pollex/photo Ben Boswell;
16 Barnaby's Picture Library; 17 Hywel
Dafydd/photo Peter Murphy; 18 William
Jones/photo Peter Murphy; 20 Andrew
Mills/photo Peter Murphy; 22 Edward
Barnsley/photos O.W. Wilmott; 23 The
Craftsman, Solva; 24 A.E. Springate;
27 Joël Degen; 28,29 W.S. Wortley/photo
Bob Jardine; 31 E.S. Iglehart; 33 Mark
Bury/photo Edward Leigh; 34 Sam
Herman; 35 Sam Herman; 36 Scottish
Tourist Board; 37 Arnold Smith;
39 S. Walton & J. Thornton; 41 Barnaby's
Picture Library; 42,43 David Cripps, Ben
Boswell; 44 Peter Murphy; 46 Marianne
Straub/Emmerich Beilon Ltd; 49
M. Sutherland; 51 Snail Trail Handweavers;
54 (top) Eric Boon/photo Peter Murphy,
(bottom) Robert Towers/Scottish Highlands
and Islands Development Board; 55 (top)
Clare Layton, (bottom) Alan Winstanley;
56 Jean Price/photo Peter Murphy;
59 M. Brandebourg; 62 Barnaby's Picture
Library; 63 Barnaby's Picture Library;
64 M. & E. Skipwith/photo Nicholas Horne
Ltd; 69 Karen Ford; 82 Frank Pratt

Compiled and designed by Paul Watkins
Editorial assistant: Elizabeth Bunster

First published in Great Britain 1983
by Sidgwick & Jackson in association
with Trusthouse Forte

Copyright © 1983 Philippa Lewis

ISBN 0-283-98914-9

Photoset by Robcroft Ltd, London WC1
Printed and bound in Great Britain
by Hazell Watson and Viney Limited,
Aylesbury, Bucks
for Sidgwick & Jackson Limited,
1 Tavistock Chambers, Bloomsbury Way,
London WC1A 2SG

Introduction The word 'craft' can mean all things to all men. It can be used simply to describe things which have been 'made by hand', but in its best sense – the one used in this book – also implies the skills and artistry of the professional craftsman.

If you think about it, everything made before the mass-manufacturing age, heralded by the Industrial Revolution, was made by craftsmen. In medieval times, the craftsmen formed themselves into guilds, powerful groups of men who, by strict rules of apprenticeship, ensured that high standards were maintained and that their numbers were never too great to devalue their skill. This system had broken down by the 17th century, but the range of techniques employed by potters, jewellers, silversmiths, glassmakers and cabinet makers continued to grow. The 18th was a particularly brilliant century. The achievements of craftsmen of that time can be seen in any of the museums with fine decorative art collections and are still preserved in the great country houses which were built and furnished during this period. However, as their work was to a large extent dictated by taste and fashion, very few craftsmen could enjoy the luxury of experimentation which is important to so much craftwork today.

The 19th century saw an immense growth in the mass production of objects for sale to an increasingly large middle class with money to spend on their homes. By the time of the Great Exhibition of 1851, over-decorated and over-elaborate work was simply pouring out from the manufacturers of Britain. The Arts and Crafts Movement emerged as a reaction to this society.

The best-known figure of the Movement is probably William Morris, but other artists, writers and architects joined him. Some banded together into guilds, following the example of the medieval craftsmen whose work they so admired. They praised those craftsmen for their truth to their material, be it wood, stone, clay or glass. This was a dramatic reaction against the fashion of the day which tended to disguise natural materials. They also considered that the work of a smith was on a par with that of a sculptor, and a woodcarver with a painter. In this spirit they searched out country craftsmen whose work had remained unchanged, and based many of their designs on such work. For instance, there was the Morris 'Sussex' chair with its rush seat and simply-turned legs, back and arms; its only decoration was the spindle turning inserted into the chairback.

During the 1970s there was a general resurgence of interest in crafts. The traditional crafts were once again sought out, preserved and admired. Woodland and coppice crafts, for example, really belong to a past way of life; their products, however, are useful and durable. The best method of making, say, wattle fences or scythe handles has evolved over hundreds of years; there is little reason to change the well-tried design or the way of making it still practised in many parts of the country. It is both fascinating and absorbing to watch such dextrous and experienced work. Younger craftsmen too, however innovative they may be, can still learn from the countrymen using the traditional methods. In this case, for example, experience can give a valuable lesson about how to work with green wood or judge the woodworking qualities of a tree that is still growing.

Other crafts developed not out of necessity, but as a useful hobby to fill in time during the otherwise unproductive winter months, with their long evenings. These tend to be decorative, such as woodcarving or needlework. Here, too, the designs and patterns have been handed down the generations, perhaps with styles typical of a particular village or town.

Both the rural skills and the decorative crafts remain a part of the craft world today. There is, however, a new approach which takes a more serious – and more experimental – view. The term 'artist craftsman' is often used in this context. Working at developing new techniques, using new, sometimes surprising, materials and often aided by modern technology, the artist craftsman aims to produce something which should be considered as a work of art. Descriptions such as 'one-off' and 'individual' are used to emphasize that this work is not one of a line of identical pots, rugs or glasses. It will be more expensive, but its creator should have given its conception correspondingly more thought and aimed for a higher quality of craftsmanship.

The renaissance of the crafts movement has given everyone the opportunity to own something that is unique, different from the run-of-the-mill manufactured object. Now, too, you have the chance to commission a piece to your own specification, for patronage need not be as expensive as it was in past centuries. If you are looking for something special, then today you may not have to travel far to find it. Although traditional craftsmen have worked near to the source of their materials, easy transport has largely changed this pattern. It is probably now more important for a craftsman to live where his work may be easily seen and sold.

Straw, rushes and willow

Basketry

In a sense basket making is one of the simplest of crafts – which is not to say that it is the easiest – for it needs very few tools. Since prehistory, baskets have been devised for an inconceivably large number of uses, each type carefully adapted in size, shape and strength for its purpose. Many, such as the Yorkshire wool-gathering baskets, have fallen from use, but even today, when the plastic bag and sack hold sway, there are at least 100 different types of basket produced in Britain. Among these are fishing creels, linen baskets, log baskets, egg baskets, cat baskets, bicycle baskets and bee skeps.

Basketry can also be part of the furniture-making process. The basket chair is a well-established country piece, and in Orkney has developed a shape and style of its own: oat straw is coiled into a rope and bound with sisal to make the characteristic hooded chairback.

In many coastal and river areas the basket maker will also make pots for lobster and crab and traps for eel and salmon. Fish traps all work on the same principle: the fish can swim into the trap with ease but escape is impossible.

Materials and methods

The most common material is willow – or as it is sometimes called, withy or osier. The low-lying areas of Somerset around Sedgemoor have the most famous osier beds, although they are also grown in Yorkshire, Essex and the Midlands. Willow rods are cut at specific times of the year: brown rods have their bark left on and are cut in winter; buff rods are made by boiling them with the bark left on, and then peeling them to leave a pale brown stain from the bark; white rods are cut in spring when the sap is just beginning to rise, enabling the bark to be easily stripped off, leaving the creamy white wood; green rods, which are used unseasoned and for the cheapest baskets, are cut all the year round.

Traditionally basket makers have used whatever trees and plants were naturally near at hand, so there are many regional variations. In low-lying marshy areas, as in parts of Norfolk, rushes were collected and woven, while sea-reeds and grasses were used on the Welsh coast and on Anglesey. Where straw was plentiful, it was coiled into ropes which were then stitched together. This produced a very dense, soft basketry useful for bee skeps (the bees then could not escape) and for cradles. Spale oak baskets were typical of Yorkshire and Lancashire; with their uprights made from rent or split oak, they were particularly used for gathering potatoes. Sussex trug baskets use willow boards overlapping like a clinker-built boat. Chips from willow logs are interwoven to make light baskets for soft fruit.

The traditional stance for a basket maker is to sit very close to the floor with a plank on his lap sloping away from him on which he rests his work. Using rods which have been well-soaked to make them pliable he always begins at the base with a 'slath'. This is the interweaving of the uprights, usually at least four in each direction. This completed, the cross-weaving is begun. It follows the basic shape of the object which

Somerset basker maker

Traditional Somerset apple pickers

is formed around a framework of rods. As one rod is used up in the cross-weaving so a new one is let in to overlap the previous. Bodkins are used to force spaces between the rods, a cleaving tool for piercing them, secateurs for cutting, sharp knives for trimming and a beating iron to knock the finished weave down tight.

Although basket makers tend to work in tried and tested shapes, some craftsmen are widening the range of materials, incorporating hedgerow plants such as wild clematis and snowberry or species of ornamental willow with different coloured stems.

Corn Dollies

People who plait straw into the intricate shapes and patterns traditional to corn dolly making almost certainly no longer believe that what they are doing is honouring Mother Earth by creating an image of her; or that

Bottle basket made from white willow rods

this idol – hence its corruption to 'dolly' – made of the summer's wheat will keep her spirit alive during the winter until the next spring's planting. But when the success of the harvest was crucial to our ancestors' well-being, perhaps even survival, it is no wonder that superstitious rituals grew up to appease the forces of nature. Many of the patterns are ancient and the names vary from place to place; for example, the straw female may be called Harvest Queen, Ceres, Demeter, Mother Earth or Corn Maiden.

Although belief in their power waned, the craft of corn dolly-making was kept alive by its inclusion in the Church's Harvest Festival celebrations. New patterns were devised which masked the pagan origins, and straw was plaited into crosses, anchors, croziers and other solidly Christian symbols. The names given to the designs evoke a picture of golden harvests all over Britain: Welsh Border Fans, Suffolk Bells, Suffolk Horseshoes, Norfolk Lanterns, Essex Terrets, Staffordshire Knots, Yorkshire Candlesticks, Devonshire Crosses, Oxford Crowns, Okehampton Mares and Kentish Ivy Maidens.

The combine harvester thrashing across the chemically-treated fields does not leave straw suitable for plaiting, nor does it leave a row of corn standing for good luck next year as the farmers used to do. Today, therefore, corn for dollies must be specially grown and reaped by hand. It needs to be long from the ear to the first joint, hollow-stemmed, unmildewed and with a full and even ear of wheat, barley or oats. The straw is worked slightly damp, so the piece should be finished at one sitting before it dries. Careful selection of stalks ensures that the dolly is neat and even.

Our forebears would have flung last year's dolly over the ploughed fields when spring came, but it is unlikely that anyone buying such carefully made decorations will do so today.

Making a corn dolly

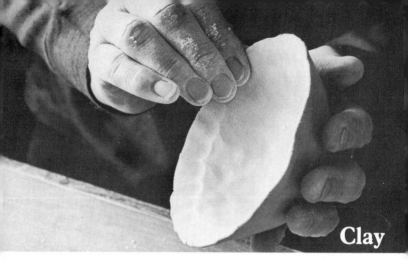

Clay

Pinch building a porcelain bowl

Pottery

In a sense, pottery is the most universal of crafts, since to make a pot one only needs clay – which is found all over the world – and fire. From such simple materials the great civilizations have produced masterpieces: Chinese and Islamic, Greek and Roman. Each style and period has contributed different techniques for making pots and decorating and glazing them. The most ancient pottery was formed by hand and hardened in an open fire.

The two vital factors in the development of the craft were the invention of the potter's wheel about 5000 years ago in the Middle East and the slow evolution of the kiln, particularly in China where 1000 years ago they fired stoneware to temperatures of 1200°C. Only by potting on a wheel could smoothly rounded shapes be formed, and only by firing in the controlled heat of a kiln could the pottery be properly glazed.

Types of Pottery

Clay is found throughout the British Isles and each area's clay will have slightly different qualities of colour, texture and content. A potter will use the sort of clay that is most suitable for the shapes, glazes and objects that he is planning. There are three main types of pottery. The simplest is **earthenware** which is very malleable and easy to use. It does not need very high temperatures (700°-1200°C) for firing, but it usually needs to be glazed all over as it is porous.

Stoneware is made from clays which can withstand a much greater heat without cracking, and once fired (at 1200°-1300°C) it becomes impermeable to liquid. Therefore it does not have to be glazed, and the body generally has a grittier appearance. **Porcelain** is a fine white clay, which is fired at the highest temperature of all (1250°-1400°C). It can be formed into thinner and more delicate shapes than earthenware or stoneware and has a translucent quality.

Methods

The usual procedure for pottery is to form the shape and then fire it. It is this firing which begins to vitrify the piece, changing the clay into a durable material. At this point the clay is often called 'biscuit', which is what it looks like. After this the glaze is put on. This is the finish made from powdered minerals and rocks (as with **enamelling**, see p. 30) – which fuses into a glassy surface when heated.

Although many people's vision of pottery is of shapes appearing almost as if by magic from the potter's wheel, a number of craftsmen use the method of **handbuilding**. They may form shapes by coiling the clay, by pinching it, by slabbing it or by press-moulding it. With any of these methods the potter can achieve effects which are not possible with a wheel: a coiled pot can be extremely large, perhaps with a very narrow neck; a pinched pot can be asymmetrical and have sculptural folds and edges; slabbed pottery, where the clay is rolled into flat sheets, can be used to make straight sides, rectangles and boxes, more as if it were wood; finally, press-moulding can produce shallow shapes with large bases that are not confined to being circular but which can be oval or square. Small decorative details can also be press-moulded, and this is usually done on a plaster of Paris mould.

Throwing is the term for making pots on a wheel. It is an intriguing skill and part of the fascination lies in the speed with which the pot can be made. The potter will 'centre' the lump of clay so that he can control the centrifugal force from the spinning wheelhead and raise the clay between his hands. When he has the shape that he wants, he cuts the clay off the wheel with a wire.

The base of the pot may need further shaping, in which case the potter waits until the clay is 'leather hard', puts it back on the wheel upside-down and then cuts away the unwanted clay with a sharp tool while slowly rotating the piece. The potter uses his skill and judgement in cutting the foot of the pot so that it conforms with the upper part and the rim. He also takes away the extra clay so that the whole piece is not too heavy. Spouts and handles are made separately by hand and then stuck on with liquid clay, often called 'slurry', at the same leather-hard stage.

Decoration

Although the potter will think of the decoration as an integral part of the pot, it is usually a separate stage which follows the making of the basic shape. While the clay is drying out, before the first firing, it is in the perfect state to carve, cut, flute or pierce, or to impress patterns. This is also the time to add applied detail: a press-moulded decoration, or a hand-modelled finial.

One of the methods of decoration often used, and which is traditionally British, involves the use of *slip*. This is liquid clay, usually cream or brown, which can be trailed in lines to make patterns or pictures. Large and splendid earthenware dishes made by the Toft family of Staffordshire in the 17th century had decoration of this kind; this was some of the earliest

Decorating a plate with slip-trailing

commemorative pottery, for the pieces often had portraits of Stuart monarchs on them.

Sgraffito decoration is when the entire piece is covered with slip and the design is then scratched through. This was a favourite ornament for the harvest jugs made in 19th-century Devon: apart from leaves, flowers, insects and geometric patterns, verses were often inscribed such as: 'Despise me not, For I am small, Fill me up And I'll please you all.'

Patterns can also be carved out of the clay and then filled with slip. This is called *inlay* and medieval tiles were decorated in this way. *Wax-resist* and *paper-resist* decoration are the terms for the effects achieved by covering the clay with either wax patterning or paper shapes before dipping it into the slip. By this method the body of the clay will show through where the wax or paper was put (since they will be burnt off during the firing). Slip decoration can be even simpler, the pot is just dipped or partially dipped into the slip.

Pigments and metal oxides may be painted directly onto the pot. This gives a lighter effect than the thick opaque slips and it generally allows for more delicate patterning.

Glazing
This is the final stage in the progress of a pot. This process is highly unpredictable, and the potter may be delighted or horrified when he removes the pots from the kiln after this final firing. Although most potters keep careful

notes of the glaze recipes and length and heat of firing, they cannot always achieve identical results. Many of the classical oriental glazes were made from simple mixtures of natural ingredients such as clay, wood ash and lime. These variable ingredients introduce elements of variety to the glaze surface. Many stoneware potters constantly experiment with new combinations of these ancient recipes. This is why the subtle shifts of colour and the spots and speckles are characteristic of craftsman-made pottery and form a contrast to the uniformity of manufactured ware. No two handmade pots can be identical. Early potters usually did not 'biscuit' fire their pots but glazed the clay directly and fired them only once. A number of contemporary potters are returning to this method for aesthetic and economic reasons.

The three essential ingredients of a glaze are mixed together to a creamy consistency with water; they are silica, a flux (as in glass) and alumina (which will thicken the melted glaze and prevent it from running off the pot during firing). Other ingredients are added for colouring. These are mainly metal oxides: iron oxide for yellows and browns, cobalt oxide for blues, and copper oxides which can give anything from metallic black to pale yellow. The colours of a glaze are further changed by the composition of the clay and by the amount of air circulating in the kiln.

Kilns can be fired by electricity, oil, gas, wood or coal, and each type of kiln produces different effects. One of the most dramatic and unpredictable methods is **salt-glazing**. This is done by throwing damp salt at intervals into a hot kiln, which reacts with the silica already present in the clay, giving a pitted textured glaze, often with a slightly iridescent sheen. It is used on stoneware and was first introduced to Britain in the 17th century.

Modelling

In the work of modern potters there is often a thin dividing line between work that is functional and pieces that are purely decorative. Onto a thrown shape of a bowl, box or teapot, the potter may add figures, animals, plants or trees. The modelling of clay is as old as making it into vessels, and many of the models that survive from ancient civilizations (recovered from burials, etc.) were used for ritual and worship.

In the history of British pottery there is a tradition of what were called 'chimney ornaments': small figures produced purely for decoration. Typical examples of these were produced by the famous 18th-century Staffordshire potters such as John Astbury and the Wood family. Often modelled from different coloured clays, they were groups of shepherds and shepherdesses, 'pew groups' (people, often musicians sitting on a bench), toby jugs, and so on. These were forerunners of the so-called 'Staffordshire figures' and 'fairings', which were slip cast and produced in quantity. Although cheerful and often brightly coloured, they lost the vitality and spontaneity of clay modelling, and it is this quality that it is good to find once more in the work of modern craftsmen.

Binding a bunch of birch twigs for a besom broom

Wood

Coppice and woodland crafts

From Britain's woodlands and forests large tree trunks of oak, elm, beech and pine went to the boat and house builders, to the carpenters, wheelwrights and cart-wrights, and to the cabinet makers. However, there still remained all the small trees and underlying wood, and it was this that generations of craftsmen converted into so many small and vitally useful objects: hurdles, brushes, rakes, clogs, fencing, walking sticks, etc.

They are collected under the loose title of 'coppice crafts' because it was by 'coppicing' trees that the craftsmen could grow the maximum amount of useful wood. Certain trees, if cut back to the root, will grow up again not with a single trunk but with a cluster of shoots, which make excellent, straight, lightweight poles. Often craftsmen would tend their own trees, carefully choosing the right time to cut the wood, usually in winter. Today there are still a few, notably the basket makers, who do this.

Some of these crafts have disappeared, such as charcoal burning. Others are fighting losing battles for survival against rapidly manufactured equivalents, or simply are no longer needed. If you

Tregaron clog-maker

shape, by steaming or by placing it in moulds of hot sand. The handle of a scythe, gently curved for the easy motion of the reaper, would be made this way, as would the curve in the handle of a walking stick. Ash would also be used for gateposts and wattle hurdles. The coppice craftsman rarely used a saw: he cut his wood with an axe and then cleaved it with a mallet and wedge.

Willow is flexible and easily split. This makes it suitable for weaving wattle, binding besom brooms, making teeth for hay rakes, or thatching spars (the pegs with which the reeds are held down). The lightness of willow meant that it was also traditionally the best wood for the milkmaid's yoke.

Birch twigs make the best brush for a besom, and although most are now bound with wire, stripped bramble or willow was formerly used. Binding hoops for barrels were usually of ash.

can seek out these craftsman-made works you will have the pleasure of knowing that what you have is a design which has been tried and tested by time, and which has been made in the same manner for perhaps hundreds of years.

Many of these craftsmen worked out of doors, in the wood itself. The tools needed are minimal – axes, adzes, billhooks, knives – and this portable workshop could be easily moved on by the workman from one coppice to the next.

The different woods

The main species of coppiced trees were ash, alder, birch, sweet chestnut, hazel and willow. Ash is a resilient wood, and it is also easy to

Clog-making

Alder and sycamore are the woods used for clog making. The traditional area of clog manufacture was Wales, which sent thousands of pairs to the industrial towns of Yorkshire and Lancashire. The uppers were of leather, but the soles were handcarved from blocks of wood using a tool unique to the trade – a clogger's knife. Attached to the workbench like a guillotine, it has a long handle – the skill of the carver lies in the leverage of the knife. Traditional clogs are still made, and although many have factory-made soles there are still a few clog makers who use traditional methods.

17

The appeal of these crafts lies partly in the careful husbandry of a valuable resource, and partly in the craftsman's thorough knowledge of the wood and its particular qualities. This comes only from years of observation and from endlessly making the same objects.

Woodcarving

Woodcarving is a skill with a long and fine tradition which takes many years to acquire. When the craft was at its height composition and plaster mouldings had yet to be perfected, so there was little alternative but to use wood or stonecarving for relief decoration. It used to be an occupation for thousands of artisans, but now there are few opportunities for the work. The ultimate virtuoso in the craft was the 17th-century wood-carver Grinling Gibbons, whose work can be seen in a number of Britain's great churches and country houses. Gibbons reached such perfection that he was able to carve from limewood a lace cravat so exquisite that it was taken for the real thing. Other examples of fine woodcarving can be seen in the vivid scenes from everyday life ornamenting medieval pew ends and misericords; 17th-century stair-cases with newel posts fashioned into baskets of fruit and flowers; delicately gilded chinoiserie on 18th-century mirror frames; gaily prancing horses on 19th-century merry-go-rounds.

Love spoons and tokens

There is another British tradition of woodcarving which belonged not to professional carvers, but to amateurs; the product of a gentler pace of life. This tradition created the intricately carved tokens of love such as the Welsh love spoon, the knitting sheaths and sticks and stay busks. The technique was relatively simple, for the carvers certainly did not have the full battery of tools which belonged to the professionals. It was usually chip-carved or pierced work, and the motifs were emblems of love and devotion such as hearts and keys.

Woods and tools

A dense, even-grained wood is the best for carving: oak, yew, lime, box, fruitwood and walnut were the favourites in the past. Today the choice has widened for the modern craftsman to include imported woods such as sapele, utile, makore and obeche from West Africa. The woodcarver's range of tools can be immense: from saws for cutting out the basic shapes to mallets and chisels and gouges in quantity. Gouges are either straight, curved or V-shaped and each slightly different shaped tool will be used to cut a different form. There are also files and scrapers and modern craftsmen will sometimes use electric drills to do some of the heavy work.

Many carvers still work in traditional areas, producing carved decoration for furniture, church fittings and signs. There has also been a revival of small domestic carvings for such things as butter moulds and bread boards. In Wales the carving of love spoons has been revived for souvenirs, though probably no one has been presented with a love spoon carved by a lover since the end of the 19th century.

Carving traditional Welsh love spoons

Turning wood on a lathe

Turning

To 'turn' a piece of wood is to rotate it on a lathe. Then by holding a chisel against it the craftsman chips away the wood, creating rounded shapes – poles, plates, bowls or any other variation on the theme. It is a technique which can show off the qualities of wood to its best advantage – highlighting the curves of the grain, the whorls of a burr and the natural colours. A wood turner makes the process appear effortless, the wood curling off the chisel as though it were cheese. His skills lie in producing good proportions through the practised combination of eye and hand. Wrong moves cannot be rectified. When the piece is finished there should be no tool marks to show how it has been made. The turned

wood is best finished with a beeswax polish which will enable it to acquire the natural patina of age and use which is so special to wood. If the object is to be used for food it will be oiled instead.

Lathes

The simplest form of lathe is a pole lathe, which is known to have existed in the pre-Christian era. This is a deceptively simple device: a belt connecting a bent sapling to a foot treadle drives a horizontal rod which spins, thus providing the necessary rotation for the turning. This sort of lathe was often set up in the woods, for example by the famous 'chair bodgers'. These craftsmen worked mainly in the beech woods of Buckinghamshire and Oxfordshire, supplying the local chair industry with roughly turned legs, stretchers and struts. In that area they were mostly working on variations of the Windsor chair, but there were similar workers in places such as the Forest of Dean and the Teifi Valley in Wales.

Lathes for ornamental turning were developed in the 17th century when all manner of elaborate forms were fashionable: spiral turning, double spiral turning, bobbin and bead and reel turning. Water power was often used for lathes, though most turners now use an electric lathe. Today there are also automatic lathes which will cut a straight pole.

Products

Small turned wood objects are often known as *treen*, and this term includes everything from tobacco jars and string holders, to lace bobbins, rattles, darning mushrooms and drinking goblets. . . . The choice of wood for these is wide: yew, lime, cherry, apple, maple, laburnum, hazel, spindle. For large-scale objects, the more usual woods are ash, beech, alder and sycamore. Sycamore is particularly popular for dairy utensils such as cream skimmers, butter churns and bowls, because it has no taste or smell.

Besides sections for furniture, the most popular products of the modern woodturner tend to be small boxes, kitchen equipment such as pepper grinders and plates and bowls. To make a bowl, the roughly shaped wood is screwed onto a revolving chuck. The exterior is cut first and then the interior. The only marks left from the lathe are the small screw-holes on the base which are then plugged.

Advances in modern adhesives have made it possible for 'sandwiches' of different coloured or stained woods to be fixed together so firmly that they can then be turned as one, and there are several craftsmen working on this theme today.

Furniture making

Before furniture making became a mechanized industry, the craftsmen were divided into joiners and cabinet makers. A joiner worked on the parts of furniture which needed his skill in jointing wood together: chairs, stools, tables and the 'carcase' or basic structure of larger pieces such as desks and chests of drawers (often called 'case' furniture). A cabinet maker was responsible for the finishing: the large expanses of wood, veneering, inlaying and so on. This gives some idea of the skills that had to be acquired. The colour, grain, feel and durability of wood are all characteristics which can be easily understood and much appreciated. Equally, though, there are problems in working with wood which the furniture maker has to take into account. For instance, while wood is strong along the length of the grain, it is weak across it; wood warps, splits and moves, and a plank may have knots and burrs, which may have the effect of weakening or cracking the structure.

The native woods which were traditionally used for furniture are oak, beech (for chairs), elm, pine, walnut and birch. Now, of course, the craftsman has no need to confine himself to these when woods are imported from all over the world.

Assembling the back of a chair and checking the diagonals for accuracy

Shaping a chair leg with a spokeshave

Tradition and innovation

There are other advantages for the furniture maker today that would have impressed and amazed the 18th-century joiner and cabinet maker. Modern adhesives are now so powerful and reliable that many of the complex and elegant joints, such as dovetails, mortises and tenons, are unnecessary. Man-made woods such as plywood, blockboard and chipboard have a flatness and stability that would never exist in a plank of, say, oak. It has always been possible to steam wood into shapes – such as a bowed chair back – but the development of laminated wood has greatly widened the scope. Equally, there are now finishes which colour, stain and shine and are impervious to heat and wet. Power tools, too, such as saws, sanders and routers, make the work much easier.

Some furniture makers are using these new materials and methods to produce radical designs and find entirely new solutions for chairs, desks and tables. However, there are some traditional designs, such

Sanding the chair seat

as the Windsor and ladderback chairs and the Welsh dresser, which have transcended fashion and style, and which furniture makers continue to make and sell. They are not 'reproduction' pieces, they have simply remained unchanged.

William Morris and other members of the Arts and Crafts Movement were among the first to appreciate these forms as fine pieces of design. The quality of a craftsman-made chair can be appreciated in the small details, such as the carefully shaped seat of a Windsor chair or the elegant details on a ladderback. There has also been a revival of interest in the old furniture-making techniques, for example working with green, unseasoned wood. The 'chair bodgers' (see Turning, p.20) turned legs and stretchers for chairs immediately after felling the tree when the wood is soft to cut. The chairs were then constructed entirely of green timber. This method can only be used with 'stick' furniture, rather than cabinet pieces, where a little instability in the finished dried-out work does not matter. To work in this manner only the basic tools of a village carpenter (made perhaps by the village blacksmith) are needed.

Decoration

Although for a period to be 'modern' meant to be undecorated, there has been an undoubted return to ornament. The methods of decorating furniture remain fundamentally the same: veneer, inlay, paint, lacquer and carving. *Veneers* are thin slivers of wood, often rare, interestingly coloured or figured, which are laid on top of more ordinary wood. *Inlays* are done with very hard woods, such as box or holly, or metal, such as brass or pewter. Plastics and resins can also be inlaid into wood. Much of the carved decoration on furniture tends to be in the styles of the Jacobean or 18th-century periods, when the work was particularly fine, but there are craftsmen today who are approaching the skill with new ideas.

Blacksmith at work on the anvil

Blacksmithing

The blacksmith was undoubtedly the most important craftsman in the community. Without his skill horses could not be shod, neither could tools be made nor farming implements mended. (Unlike so many other crafts, forging iron is not one at which the amateur can easily try his hand and achieve instant results.) However, progress in the 20th century has slowly whittled away the smith's traditional ground.

Many smiths still work to designs that might have been first produced 100 or 200 years ago, and they work with equipment that

Metal

equally has seen little change – fire, anvil, hammer. Yet, as with so many crafts in recent years, there has been a great revival of interest in and a desire to use iron in new ways, and to experiment with new forms. One reason for this burst of creativity has been the adoption of tools and ways of working previously used in industry, and these allow the blacksmith much greater freedom. For example, the power hammer has increased the size and quantity of work that a blacksmith can produce single-handed; the electric arc-welder and oxyacetylene cutter make cutting and welding iron much simpler processes and reduce dependence on the forge hearth.

Materials and Methods

Despite all these advances the fundamental skill of the blacksmith remains the same: the knowledge of how to work iron and steel. Most smiths today use mild steel, which contains a percentage of carbon. It is produced in vast quantities for the engineering industry and can be bought in sheets, bars, rods, tubes, angles, and so on. Less commonly used is wrought iron, which is purer but far more expensive to manufacture. Its advantages are that it can be worked at a wider range of temperatures and is easier to forge into delicate and intricate patterns.

The magic of iron is that this material, valued by man for thousands of years for its great strength, becomes as soft as clay when heated and can be shaped and cut. If two pieces are hammered together when hot, they fuse perfectly. The blacksmith heats the iron in his fire and watches the colour of the metal intently as it turns from black through red to white hot. He knows from experience at what colour the metal is best worked. He cannot leave the metal too long in the fire or it begins to burn and form lumps.

The heart of the forge is the fire, usually of coke or coal but occasionally gas-fuelled. No longer is it the job of the blacksmith's assistant to work the bellows to blow the fire to the right intensity; this is now usually done by electric centrifugal blowers.

The anvil, on which the smith works the hot iron, is of a shape which has been evolved by generations of ironworkers. It is made of a block of iron or steel with a smooth, specially hardened surface. It is mounted on a heavy block of wood to absorb the shock of the hammer-blows. On the top surface there is a punching or 'pritchet' hole – a small circle which will receive the point of any tool being used to punch holes into hot iron. There is also a square hole or 'hardie' hole into which anvil tools can be fitted. The most important anvil tools are the 'hardie' which is a chisel to split or cut, the 'swage' which is a simple mould or die, and 'stakes' which are miniature anvils for forging different shapes. The tools with which a smith works on the molten metal are hammers, punches, tongs and chisels. These come in an enormous variety of shapes, weights and sizes, each one designed for a different purpose.

When the work is completed on the anvil the hot metal is plunged into the water trough with an unforgettable sizzle and puff of steam. When the iron is cold there is further work to do on it. It may be cut with saws, or drilled with notches and holes. Smooth shapes and finishes were done with files and emery, but now smiths often use grinding and sanding wheels. Pieces may also be screwed, riveted, bolted or collared together with small metal loops.

Iron remains strong only as long as it is protected. A damp atmosphere will corrode it, gradually reducing it to rusting flakes. Traditionally iron was painted for protection, but it may now be galvanized (dipped into molten zinc), electro-plated (covered with a thin film of copper, nickel, chromium or zinc), flame metallized (sprayed with the same metals in a molten state), or just protected with lacquer or wax.

In the 19th century the development of cast iron meant that very elaborate and fanciful designs could be easily made; this dealt a death blow to much beautiful and skilled hand-forged work. Now cast iron itself is so expensive it is a good time to look again at the work of the blacksmith: gates, railings, balconies, weather-vanes, fire-backs, fire-baskets and light and lamp holders are still things that are often best handmade in iron.

Jewellery

Man has always recognized the intrinsic beauty of gold and silver. From the earliest civilizations, they have been formed into objects of self-adornment. Rich hoards of gold jewellery – hair ornaments, earrings, chains, necklaces and finger-rings – were found when the ancient city of Ur in Mesopotamia was excavated, and these were made about 2500 BC. Stones such as brilliantly blue lapis lazuli, dark red carnelian and patterned agates were also used from this early time.

Gradually, craftsmen learned to cut stones with many facets in order to achieve a glitter and sparkle from the refraction of light. As Europeans explored other continents so they brought back precious stones: emeralds from South America, rubies from Burma, sapphires from Ceylon, opals from Australia and diamonds from India, Brazil and South Africa. The rarity of these stones and the subsequent value put on them has meant that jewellery has often been used to proclaim the wealth of the wearer and even as currency.

Materials and methods

Nevertheless, jewellers have always experimented with other cheaper materials, most of which have required skill in their manufacture. In past centuries cut and faceted steel, very finely cast iron, horse-hair, shells and porcelain have all been intricately worked. The escalating price of precious metals and stones has meant that the modern jeweller has once again searched out new and cheaper materials. Modern technology has brought new metals to the fore such as titanium, niobium and tantalum – when heated or electrolytically anodized they take on iridescent oil-slick colours. Unlike more traditional metals, however, they are not malleable and are impossible to solder or form into complex shapes. The jeweller's skill is shown by the colourings achieved and the shapes cut.

Synthetic materials – perspex, plastic resin, nylon filaments, acrylics, polyester – are used to make jewellery which has a new range of bright colouring not found in the natural world. Sometimes these are combined with gold and silver and sometimes used alone, but they do enable craftsman-made jewellery to be within the price range of everyone. Bone, ivory, ebony, mother of pearl, shell, glass (see p. 31), enamel (see p. 30), ceramics, tortoiseshell, and even feathers, are some of the other materials used in modern jewellery to achieve the wide variety of effect.

The jeweller buys gold and silver in several forms: in sheets, wire, tubes or grain. He creates his shapes in two basic ways. The first method is to build up the piece by sawing the shapes and pieces, and

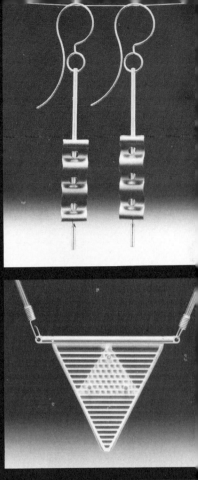

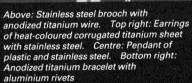

Above: Stainless steel brooch with anodized titanium wire. Top right: Earrings of heat-coloured corrugated titanium sheet with stainless steel. Centre: Pendant of plastic and stainless steel. Bottom right: Anodized titanium bracelet with aluminium rivets

bending and hammering. Finally the piece is polished and then soldered together. Gold and silver are made malleable by the process of *annealing*, that is heating the metal and then allowing it to cool.

The second method is casting. This is a technique also widely used in silversmithing (see below) to achieve complicated sculptural or figurative forms. Grain gold and silver are used in casting, the method by which most mass-produced jewellery is made.

Silversmithing

Every piece of silver and gold made and sold in Britain is checked for purity. The hallmark is the proof of this – a remarkable practice which dates back as far as the 14th century. Each coffee pot, fork, salt cellar and candlestick is sent to the assay offices in London, Birmingham, Sheffield or Edinburgh. When the silver is found to be of the right standard four marks are put onto it: the **assay mark** for whichever town inspected it, the maker's mark, the standard mark for silver or gold and a letter which is the code for the year.

Few craftsmen have the opportunity to work in solid gold, but silver shares most of its characteristics and both metals are worked in the same manner. Their qualities lie in their ductility and malleability, which mean that they lend themselves well to a wide variety of manufacturing techniques. Proof of this can be seen in the works of extraordinary complexity produced in past centuries; from the fine detail of a medieval

salt cellar, fashioned perhaps in the form of a sailing ship, to the wild rococo fantasies of waves, rocks, shells and chinamen heaped onto an 18th-century teapot. Gold and silver also share the quality which has led them to be so universally prized, that of their gleaming surface. Gold does not tarnish or discolour, and while silver does tarnish, it also acquires a lustrous patina through age and use.

Methods

There are two traditional methods of silversmithing: either to forge and hammer the silver into shape and then solder it together, or to melt it and cast it into shape. It can also be worked on a lathe, a technique known as 'spinning', and it can be pressed or stamped into shape, but both these methods, developed in the 19th century, are those of mass-production and aimed at producing multiples.

To make a hollow vessel the silver is 'raised'. This means that a flat sheet is hammered into shape over stakes and heads in doming

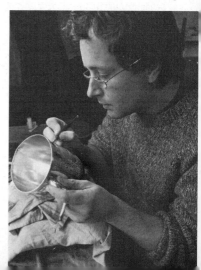

Engraving a silver cup

blocks or round mandrels – the heavy steel tools which guide the shape of the hammered silver. The silversmith will try to keep the surface as smooth as possible during this process, but after the shaping a piece is worked over with a planishing hammer to remove all tool marks and leave it ready for polishing.

Rims, bases and handles are often made from silver wire (the term is rather misleading, since it may be quite thick) which is often shaped by pulling it through a drawplate. A length of silver wire, one end of which is tapered, can be simply drawn through the shaped holes in a steel die; this compresses the metal, thus changing its shape and reducing its size as it is squeezed through. As the silversmith works, he must anneal the silver by heating it. This will soften it and prevent it becoming hard and cracking. After annealing and soldering the silver is cleaned by plunging it into an acid bath – a process known as 'pickling'.

The oldest method of casting silver is called the lost wax process (sometimes known by its French name, *cire perdu*). The pattern is modelled in wax which is then immersed in plaster; when this has set hard the wax is melted out, leaving a mould into which the molten metal can be poured. Rubber moulds often replace this technique now. Only by casting can complicated three-dimensional detail be made, or relief sections which can then be applied to the main body of the work.

Decorative techniques
The decorative techniques are, in the main, the same as they have been for hundreds of years. To decorate with embossed (*repoussé*) ornament the flat metal is hammered on the wrong side, which stretches it, curving it outwards on the right side. This technique is often used in conjunction with chasing, where the metal is indented on the right side by steel punches lightly knocked with a hammer. For example, the chasing might outline the petals of an embossed flower.

To *engrave* silver a sharp tool is used to gouge out a line of metal, leaving a fine, bright edge in contrast to the smooth silver. A new development in the 19th century was *electrotyping*, which is a method of reproducing minute detail. This method is still used, mainly in manufacturing, to achieve a textured finish. Fine *piercing* of silver can also be a form of decoration; it is delicate work done with a tiny saw blade.

Much of the work of the silversmith lies in finishing the surface. This involves patient polishing, first with fine abrasives and then with soft bobs and mops which are made of leather, cotton and wool.

Enamelling

The beauty of enamelling lies in the combination of the metal – copper, silver, gold – and the colours of the enamel, often brilliant and glistening, sometimes subtle and opaque. It is an ancient art which was practised by the Greeks, Chinese, Byzantines and Celts, among others.

Enamelling involves applying a thin coat of powdered glass to a metal surface and then firing it in a kiln so that the glass fuses onto the metal with a hard, bright, shiny surface. Part of the craftsman's skill lies in the preparation of his glazes. Whether he grinds the glass to a powder himself or buys it ready made, it must be carefully washed to achieve a fine clear colour. He combines silica (glass) with lead oxides and borax to control the softness or hardness of the enamel, which must obviously melt faster than the metal base. Potash and soda give sparkle to the finish and metal oxides provide the colour. Gold oxide produces red, manganese makes purple, tin white, uranium yellow, copper turquoise, and so on.

Techniques

There are several recognizable enamelling techniques. The two oldest methods are *champlevé* and *cloisonné*. With *champlevé*, troughs are engraved in the metal base plate into which the enamel glaze is placed and then fired to produce solid colour. Successive layers of colours may then be laid on the first. The pattern for *cloisonné* is made with thin metal walled compartments which are then filled with enamel. The effect after firing is that each colour is divided from the next by a thin metal line. This method is the basis of the *plique à jour* technique which has the effect of a stained glass window. This is achieved by etching away the metal base so that the enamel is transparent. The term *basse-taille* describes the method in which the metal base is engraved in low relief so that when the enamel is laid over the top it is emphasized by the differing depths of the enamel.

Enamels can also be applied to glass and ceramics by the same process of fusing the powdered glass to the surface. Sometimes resins are laid onto metal, a method which is known as 'cold enamelling' – but this is a misnomer. True enamelling involves the skill of fusing the glass to metal.

Enamelling, now as in earlier periods, is mostly used on small objects – jewellery, small boxes and bowls.

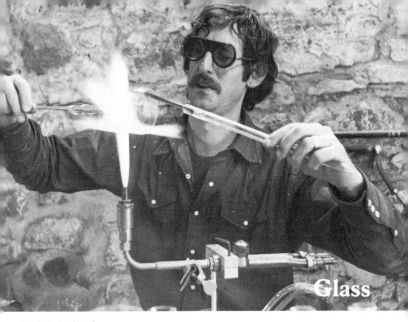

Manipulating hot glass

Glass

Like so many inventions, the discovery of glass was probably fortuitous. By about 1500BC, however, a gradual understanding of how best to make glass was developing. Sand, when mixed with soda and lime and heated to a high temperature, produces glass. It was considered a precious material, and many of the methods of working it, such as grinding and polishing, were the techniques used for semi-precious stones and precious metals.

For another 1000 years, until the technique of blowing was evolved, hollow vessels could only be made around a 'core' (probably sand and cloth) which was removed after the glass had cooled. This was soda glass which is hard and brittle. At the end of the 17th century the soda ash was replaced by lead oxide, and a softer, clearer glass resulted. This also had the added advantage of taking longer to cool and therefore being easier to work.

Craftsmen in glass can be divided into several categories, each one demanding different skills and with different methods of working. Closest to the volatile and dramatic nature of the material are those who work with 'hot glass', taking the fiery molten glass and cajoling it into shapes. In contrast there is the cool, delicate and precise work of the glass engraver and finally those working with flat glass, traditional leaded stained glass, or using more modern techniques of glass appliqué and texturing. There are also a growing number of studio glassmakers who use kilns to form the glass. At low temperatures (650°-800°C) the glass can be fused, stretched and bent, but at higher temperatures (up to 950°C) it will flow and can, for example, be cast like metal.

Hot glass

In terms of the craft revival, working with hot glass is comparatively recent. The reasons for this are not hard to see: whereas it is relatively easy for a potter to set up a workshop, the physical difficulties of producing glass are more daunting and the equipment more elaborate and expensive. Usually, therefore, several craftsmen work together in a glasshouse sharing the large cost of running a furnace.

Glassmaking is spectacular to watch: the heart of the workshop is the furnace, and into its roaring depths the glassmaker dips a hollow pole, an 'iron', and draws out a blob or 'gather' of molten glass, glowing red hot. The glass is shaped with wet wooden moulding implements while it is rolled backwards and forwards to keep it symmetrical. By blowing down the iron it is hollowed and expanded. As he works, the craftsman must keep returning the piece to the furnace so that the glass stays hot and malleable.

The final shaping is usually done with long tongs, known as 'jacks'. The piece is finally separated from the blowing iron by connecting a steel rod or 'pontil' to the base of it while the rim is then completed. When the pontil rod is removed it leaves a rough mark (a pontil mark) on the underside of the piece which will always tell you that it has been made by hand. Hot glass can also be cast and moulded, pressed and centrifuged, or the various techniques may be combined, as in blown moulded glass, which was very popular in the early 19th century.

Decorative techniques

In addition to the blowing, stretching, pinching, building and piercing required to make the final form of the piece of glass, some colouring techniques also take place while the glass is molten. Rods of coloured glass can be trailed and feathered on to produce inlaid patterns when the glass is blown or rotated. Coloured oxides and enamels can also be added. Iridescent colours can be given by introducing metal salt fumes. Numerous other decorative techniques can be used while the glass is hot. For instance, by pricking the glass with damp wooden spikes, hollow threads of air or bubbles can be embedded within the walls of the glass. All hot glass must be annealed to prevent stress building up within the glass and causing it to shatter when cold. This is done by allowing it to cool down at a controlled rate.

Glass engraving, cutting and etching

Once glass is cold, there are many more processes by which the craftsman can put his mark on a piece. Usually this is by **cutting** or **engraving**. The most powerful tool used in this process is the wheel-engraver. To cut lead crystal, stone or carborundum wheels are used, followed by soft polishing wheels. Engraving is done with a small copper wheel used with abrasives to achieve a range of intricate and fine effects. All wheel-engraving, however, tends to give pieces a bold, sculptural look and it is usually done on heavy lead glass.

Some glass engravers use hand-held diamond or tungsten carbide tools which give a more delicate, ethereal line. The design is either drawn on, or stippled with tiny dots, a method evolved by the Venetians for their thin brittle soda glass. Drills similar to those used by dentists are the third type of engraving tool. They are probably the most adaptable because they have a flexible drive and can be moved over the surface of the glass.

The principle of etching is easily translated onto glass and this method was developed in the 19th century. A wax layer covers the glass and the design is scratched through, so that when the glass is dipped in acid, the acid will eat into the exposed glass. Different acids produce different effects on glass. Sand-blasting is another method; this enables glass craftsmen to create a matt, textured finish. It can also be used to 'carve' glass.

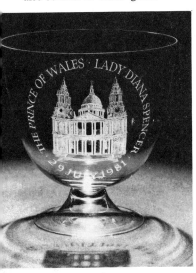

Engraved glass commemorating
Royal Wedding

Stained glass

When the rich and glowing stained glass was made by the medieval craftsmen for the cathedrals and churches of Europe, no one had solved the problem of how to make large sheets of glass. It was difficult to make pieces larger than about two feet square by the methods then known (blowing and then flattening the glass). It was only by linking pieces .together with lead that the giant Gothic windows could be glazed. It was also natural that in making these special windows craftsmen should use the most brilliant and rare colours.

Glass can be 'stained' in various ways: oxides can be added to the molten glass so that the colour is solid throughout; or it can be 'flashed' by laying a thin layer of coloured glass on top of the clear. Designs can be painted on with a powdered glass paste then fused into the glass by firing – the same technique as enamelling on metal.

The Victorian Gothic Revival gave stained glass a new lease of life; it was seen as a medium suited for secular as well as ecclesiastical use. Art Nouveau designers recognized electric light as a natural partner to stained glass and produced leaded light fittings with flowing plant designs.

Today, although the problem of making very large sheets of glass has long been overcome, the craft of stained glass still has its place in architecture. Glass windows and panels now have much more varied surfaces and textures with glass appliqué laminations, sand-blasting, silvering and acid-etching joining more traditional techniques.

Taking molten glass from furnace and (below) shaping it

Left: Studio glass

Horn

Raw material of a Scottish hornworker

Hornwork

For our Celtic ancestors, the horn was a powerful symbol denoting power and fertility; the gods that they worshipped were horned and they drank out of horn cups. The unchanged shape of a horn has frequently been used for drinking cups and powder horns, but as a material it is also extremely malleable, with many useful qualities. When steamed and heated horn becomes pliable, and can be slit, pressed into a flat sheet and moulded into shape. It is finally buffed to a natural shine. Horn was an immensely useful material to our predecessors, for it could be made into cups, spoons, boxes and so on, which were often valued highly enough to be trimmed with silver.

In Britain three different types of horn have been used. In past centuries, cow horn was the most valued; its colouring ranges from black to a creamy white and its texture is smoother than other horns.

Like tanneries, hornworks tended to gather near the drovers' routes, the well-worn roads along which the fattened cattle and sheep were driven to the cities. Sheep horns are not as adaptable as cow horns, often having a gnarled and craggy surface. However, they are traditionally used for shepherds' crooks ('cromachs' or 'cleeks' in Scotland). The ram of the Blackface sheep is supposed to provide the best horn for this, and the horn will be carefully worked until exactly the right curve necessary for catching sheep by the neck is achieved.

Staghorn is really only worked in Scotland. The stag sheds his antlers every year and a 'royal' stag will have as many as 12 points on each. The straight points are often used for knife and fork handles and the solid sections of horn (the tips) can be sliced for buttons. When Queen Victoria, after her sojourns at Balmoral, led the nation in wild enthusiasm for things Scottish, staghorn was popular for jewellery, for candelabra – and even for furniture decoration.

Horn is no longer much used and its products tend to be directed towards the tourist industry. Also, sadly in these days of de-horned cattle, much of the raw material has to be imported.

Punching decoration on leather

It is possible to imagine, in an age of plastics, that leather is redundant. Substitutes could probably be found for all the many uses to which leather has been put in the past. But substitutes do not have the indefinable quality of leather, the feel, the smell, the range of finishes, the extraordinary variety that the craftsman can give to this material.

Until man had discovered how to prevent animal hides rotting, their use was limited. But once knowledge of tanning had spread, the working of leather became one of the most commonly practised crafts: for boot and shoemaking, for saddlery and harness, for clothing, upholstery, screens and wallcoverings, for baggage and perhaps more surprisingly, for pitchers, cups and jugs (after moulding and forming).

Preparing the leather
Like hornworkers, tanners traditionally congregated near the cattle and sheep drovers' routes and the large animal markets. The fellmonger (as the skin and hide dealer is also called) preserves the leather in two basic ways. **Vegetable tanning** involves leaving the skin once it has been scraped, de-haired and split, to soak in a tannin solution. Tree bark, best of all oak, is the most common source

of tannin, but it is also present in other plants. **Mineral tanning** involves the use of alum and, less often, chrome, and will produce leather with different qualities and characteristics. Other leather treatments include the pounding of oil and fat into chamois leather to make it supple or soaking, stretching and drying taut to get the stiffness of rawhide, vellum or parchment. For sheepskin the fleece is obviously left intact and washed, while the hide is preserved in the usual manner.

Tools and methods

The tools for working leather are relatively simple. Cutting is done with a variety of knives – the one most distinctive to the craft being a half-moon shape with a sharp edge all around. Punches or stitch wheels are used to mark and make equidistant and straight lines of stitching. The stitch wheel works like a pastry-cutter, marking as it is wheeled along. The thread is waxed to make it hard and resilient.

Much of the beauty of leather lies simply in its polished finish, but it can be decorated in other ways. Patterned metal punches, for instance, sometimes heated to shine and slightly scorch the leather, produce a low-relief decoration. This method is sometimes used in conjunction with gilding for traditional bookbindings. Equally, the surface can be embossed by applying heated pressure on dampened leather. Rather in the same manner as marquetry with wooden veneers, work can be inlaid with leathers of different colours and grains. Many leather craftsmen will dye their own skins to get a wide range of

colouring and there are new methods of silk-screening patterns onto suede. When leather is soaked in cold water it is easily moulded into shape and will retain the shape if it is then pressed and heated.

Leatherwork

Bags, purses, cases and belts are the stock-in-trade of most leather-workers. These objects use leather to its best advantage. In some cases the craftsmen working in this field may have started off making saddles and bridles before the decline in that trade. Many of the techniques are shared: for example, the strong saddle-stitching where two threads are used, as on a sewing machine; methods of attaching buckles; and the edging lines made with a hot iron.

Saddlery and harness making

This is a craft which is past its heyday. When horses were the major means of transport, saddles, bridles and harness would have been needed not only for riding horses, but also for the workhorse pulling everything from coaches to canal boats – almost anything on wheels. The demand has diminished since then, and the work has become much simpler: for example, a 19th-century cavalry officer's bridle was a very elaborate affair. However the competitive spirit of much of today's riding has ensured that the craft has not fossilized but is experimenting with new patterns and materials. Racing

38

Leather craftsman using a hole puncher

saddles are made to weigh only a few ounces, polo saddles have a reinforced 'tree' or frame, to stand up to the strain of the rider moving around, and show jumping and eventing saddles are designed to keep the rider leaning forward.

The saddle

The saddle tree was traditionally made from carved beechwood, but to reduce weight it is now usually made from laminated wood, or even carbon fibre. Over this webs are stretched to make a firm but springy seat. It is then padded with wool, horsehair or plastic foam, and covered in leather, usually pigskin. The skirts and flaps are sewn on, and then the panel which is the underpart of the saddle and which raises it off the horse's backbone.

Harness

The harness is made in three parts: the collar against which the horse pulls, the pads which support the weight of the shafts and the bridle and strapwork which join the whole together. Unlike saddlery, the demand for harnesses is naturally very limited but, like saddlery, their manufacture is skilled work. The collar is the most difficult part to make. The inner part, which goes against the horse's neck, is the 'wale', of leather tightly packed with rye straw; outside this is the body of the collar which is also leather, stuffed with straw and flock. Between the two are attached the 'hames' – metal fittings to which the rest of the harness is fitted. Harnesses for shows are often made of patent leather, a special process whereby the leather has been sprayed with lacquer.

Boot and shoemaking

Craftsmen do still exist who make boots and shoes by hand, though the work tends to be mainly in the field of orthopaedic footwear. However, there are still people who are happy to pay for the luxury and comfort of a boot or shoe made to fit their feet exactly. Riding boots are often handmade because they have to fit not only the foot but the calf. A manufacturer cannot afford to produce all the variations in even this apparently small field: from boots of box calf (so-called originally because the black colour came from the berries of box trees) with patent leather tops for dressage; to tougher wax calf boots for hunting (finished with a liquid blacking which is then 'boned' – rubbed with deer bone to close the surface of the leather and give a glossy finish). The soles of handmade footwear may be of the best oak-bark tanned leather which is tough and long-wearing. This is usually from the animal's back where the hide is thicker and stronger.

A craftsman-made boot or shoe will be a perfect fit. After the feet are carefully measured, the lastmaker carves a replica of each foot in beech or maple wood, and it is round this model that the shoes or boots are made. The measurements are converted into a paper pattern and the sections are cut by the 'clicker', the leather cutter. The 'closer' then joins the seams and finally sews on the soles around the wooden last. These jobs can obviously be done by one man,

Saddlemaker at work

there are still many craftsmen bookbinders who give each book individual treatment.

Binding a book by hand is a lengthy process involving stitching the pages, preparing and covering the boards, attaching the endpapers and finishing. Over the centuries a traditional style of leather bookbinding has evolved which has changed little since the Renaissance: the decoration is tooled and gilded (with leather punches and gold leaf), the silk headband and tailband protect and decorate the top and bottom of the spine, the covers are given roll or fillet borders and there are raised horizontal bands (covering the cords onto which the pages are sewn) down the length of the spine. Inside one of these panels on the spine is a leather label on which the title and author's name are blocked in gold letters. Especially beautiful papers are used as endpapers – often they are hand-marbled. As a book will often outlive its binding, there will always be a demand for this traditional craft.

but traditionally they were often separate operations.

Most handmade boots and shoes follow traditional patterns: such as riding boots, brogues and walking boots. To take such care may seem unwarranted with shoes that rapidly become unfashionable. As with all traditional crafts that appear to belong to a society that has almost ceased to exist, there is, however, an element of rediscovery. Bored with the products of mass-manufacture, there are now craftsmen to make and the clients to buy interesting and original handmade shoes.

Bookbinding

Before cloth binding was introduced in the 19th century, the standard binding for books was leather. The bindings of most books are now mass-produced but

Modern Approaches

There is a new movement among craftsmen who feel that this basic process should be applied to some more adventurously designed bookbindings. They have moved away from the traditional styles and believe that the decoration of the binding should illustrate or relate to the theme of the text, or perhaps even stand as a beautiful object in its own right. To this end they employ a wide variety of decorative techniques apart form the usual one of gold tooling. The basic binding material is still usually leather or vellum.

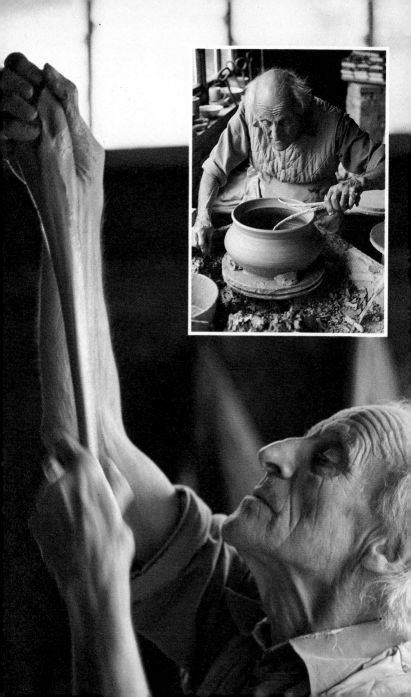

Michael Cardew throwing a bowl and (below) decorating a jug

Opposite: Michael Cardew pulling a handle and (inset) measuring for a casserole lid   43

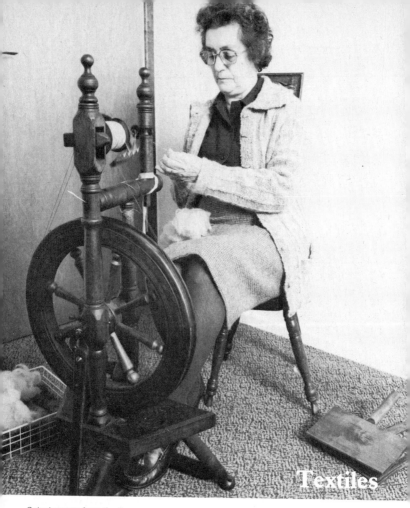

Spinning yarn from the fleece

Spinning

In areas where sheep grazed, almost every home in the past would have had a spinning wheel for converting the thick oily mass of a fleece into strong, even yarn.

This calm and peaceful process,

traditionally the province of the women ('When Adam delved and Eve span . . . '), is not strictly necessary in this machine age, but many weavers and knitters like using handspun yarn. This can be designed exactly for the work that the craftsman plans, and can make the most of the immensely varied texture and sheen that occur in the wool of sheep, let alone in other more unusual animal fibres such as Angora goat, Angora rabbit, cashmere, alpaca, camel hair, and even dog and cow hair. There is an almost infinite variety of yarns which can be made by hand spinning, whereas the choice from manufacturers tends to get smaller. For example, fibres can be spun with deliberate unevenness to give a knobbly texture or with mixed colours to give variegated yarns.

Preparing the wool
Before spinning can be started, the fleece has to be carefully prepared. It may be washed or spun in its natural oils, but a good even yarn can only be made if the 'staple' (the natural length of a fibre) is sorted and separated; there may be as many as six different types of wool on one fleece. It is this sort of time-consuming care that can only be taken with handspinning; manufacturers will frequently mix them all together and this produces wool of inferior quality.

Different breeds of sheep naturally produce wool with different characteristics. Mountain and hill breeds, such as those bred in the Welsh mountains and the Lake District, produce a medium staple; Kent breeds, Border Leicester, Lincoln and Devon Longwools provide, as the last name suggests, a long staple wool which is sometimes semi-lustrous; and a short, soft, springy wool comes from the downland sheep of Sussex, Dorset and Hampshire.

After sorting, the wool must be 'teased'. This involves careful disentangling of knots, removing bits and pieces embedded in the fleece and gently pulling the fibres apart

from one another. The next stage is 'carding'. This is done with special combs called 'carders', made of thin metal pins set into wood, cloth or leather. After the wool has been carefully passed through the carders it is rolled into a wad (known as a 'rolag') and is then ready to spin.

The spinning wheel
The simplest device for spinning is a weighted spindle twisted by hand. The basic types of spinning wheels are those whereby the horizontal spindle is driven by a hand-turned wheel fitted with a strap. The more sophisticated is a flyer wheel which has the advantage of being worked by a treadle, which allows the spinner to have both hands free to manipulate the yarn. It also winds the finished yarn directly onto a bobbin. The skill in spinning which, like so many craft skills, looks deceptively easy, lies in a sensitive hand that draws the wool out as it is twisted and instinctively keeps it at an even thickness with the same amount of twist throughout.

There are various ways of spinning, but the two principal ones are *woollen* and *worsted*. The first gives a warmer, rougher looking, more elastic yarn and the second a smoother, shinier, cooler yarn. Greater strength and variety may be given to the yarn by 'plying', which means twisting together two or more yarns; these may be different colours or fibre or twists. This is done on the spinning wheel.

When wound into a hank the yarn can be taken a further stage – dyeing – or it may simply be washed and used in its natural state.

Overleaf: Handweaving on a 16-shaft loom

Dyeing yarns

Many weavers and knitters dye their own yarns. In this way they can immeasurably widen the range of colours to work with, and can get exactly the right colour. Synthetic dyes were introduced in the middle of the 19th century and textile manufacturers were very quickly seduced by their bright colour range and constant colour values. They were much easier to use than their predecessors, natural dyes, which sometimes involved painstaking gathering of material from all over the countryside and which could produce erratic results. With vegetable dyeing, such minutiae as the time of year the plant was gathered or the softness or hardness of the water may change a colour. Some plants were especially cultivated for dyeing – weld for yellow, woad for blue, St John's Wort for yellow, and of course onion skins for yellow and orange. The use of natural dyes dates back to prehistory – our ancestors, for instance, dyed themselves blue with woad. By the 1930s, when interest was revived, many of the old recipes for dyeing had been lost, and were no longer handed down through families of dyers. Experiments are now being made to rediscover them.

So-called 'substantive' dyes are those which are permanent on their own: for example the yellows, browns and reds from lichens. Most natural dyes are 'adjective' which means that they need the addition of a 'mordant' to bring out the colour and fix it in the yarn. These are chemicals, from alum, tin, chrome, iron and copper. The plants and trees are all around us: for red – birch bark, and sorrel and potentilla roots; for blue – dog's mercury, yellow iris, sloeberries; for yellow – agrimony, ash, birch leaves, bracken tips and roots, pear and plum leaves; for brown – alder, larch, walnut, waterlily root; and for purple – bryony, dandelion roots, and oak bark and acorns. Mixing extends the range: for instance, yellow and blue dyes are used consecutively to make green.

It is possible to dye wool in the fleece but it is usually done after spinning. First it is thoroughly cleaned or 'scoured' to remove all grease and then it is put into the dye vat in a hank. The craftsman will obviously be thinking about the ultimate design as he dyes his yarns, but none more so than those working in the **ikat** technique (see p. 52).

Cotton and linen are harder to dye than wool and silk, and they are more often dyed with synthetic dyes.

Weaving

Weaving is one of the most ancient of crafts; like pottery it was born of necessity – in this case to make clothing. At the simplest level, weaving is just the interlacing of threads at right angles to one another, but as to be expected with anything that has been done for several thousands of years, it has developed many elaborations. Machines and power looms apart, the hand loom comes in many different shapes and sizes, from the small **inkle loom** (see p. 52) to make perhaps a metre of braid, to a large vertical tapestry loom at which

Weaving tweed in the Scottish Highlands

several weavers can work simultaneously. Equally, the different arrangements of yarns and threads can produce weaves of different effects. Wool, cotton, linen and silk are the most common threads to weave, but raffia, sisal, jute, camel hair, horsehair, mohair, even plastic film, grass, slivers of wood and feathers are among materials incorporated by weavers today.

Tapestry

This term describes a particular method of weaving, usually for wall-hangings. Tapestries are woven on frame looms, which are either vertical or horizontal. Historically, they combined the functions of wall insulation, draught-exclusion and, perhaps most important of all, decoration. Tapestries preceded oil paintings, engravings, etchings and watercolours, and those who could not afford them even painted canvas or linen in imitation of them. Unlike other weaving techniques, the *weft* (the threads which are woven horizontally) never runs through all the *warp* (the static vertical threads), but is worked in small sections according to the colour. Each area will be woven with a bobbin of a separate colour, which is why tapestries will sometimes have slits in them where the colour has changed.

After falling from fashion in the 18th and 19th centuries, the art of tapestry was revived at the end of the 19th century by William Morris, and it has slowly developed since then. For centuries tapestries have been woven from cartoons made from paintings. The object was to reproduce the painting as faithfully as possible from the cartoon, which was placed behind the tapestry while it was being woven. Famous artists' works that have been chosen range from Raphael to Henry Moore.

In recent years many artists have begun not only to design tapestries but to weave them themselves, and that has led to greater innovation and greater freedom. New techniques have been invented, traditional ones employed in new ways, and primitive ones rediscovered. Many of the new tapestries are three dimensional – more like soft sculpture.

Fabrics

Scotland and Wales have long traditions of hand-loom weaving; many cottages and crofts had looms at which members of the family would work during the winter months or in the evenings when there was no agricultural work to be done. In Scotland plaids and tweeds were the typical cloths, and in Wales decorative blankets, known as 'carthenni', which have the characteristic double cloth weave, were woven.

Unlike tapestry which can be woven on a simple frame loom, more sophisticated looms are needed for lengths of frabric and for rugs. Small pieces of weaving, such as bags, small hangings and cushion covers, are often made on a table loom, but this is slow to use as the shafts have to be raised and lowered by hand. On a simple loom there are two shafts which will lift every alternate thread leaving a gap or 'shed' through which the shuttle holding the weft is passed. Most serious weavers will have a floor loom, which makes weaving much faster as the feet work the shafts, leaving both hands free to work the weft. These larger looms will keep the work even, store the finished cloth and allow the weaver to work up a regular speed and rhythm which is essential for good weaving.

To produce a plain weave you need only two shafts. This will produce the standard one-up, one-down interlacing. The craftsman weaver can elaborate this very simple theme by weaving fabric warp-faced, where only the warp shows on the finished fabric, or weft-faced, where only the weft shows (as in tapestry), or by using both alternately which is called 'cramming and spacing'. The threads can also be manipulated to produce gauze effects.

For patterned weaves, such as twills, herringbone, honeycomb or double cloth, four or more shafts are needed to vary the lifting of the warp, for example over-two and under-one interlacing. For these, more complex looms such as the counter-balanced, countermarch and dobby are used. A dobby loom has a simple programming system, but with the other types the weaver must remember the sequence in which the shafts are lifted and work the corresponding pedals with his feet.

Given the variety of yarns that it is possible to use, the subtle patternings of different weaves, and the almost infinite range of colouring, from both natural and synthetic dyes, then the possibilities for handwoven cloth are immense. Unlike mass-produced fabrics, small lengths can be woven to a particular width, and patterns, stripes and checks can be woven so that when the garment is made up they will appear in the right place.

In Scotland, in particular, a surprisingly large amount of tweed is still handwoven. For example, Harris tweed is guaranteed by the

Tapestry being woven on an upright loom

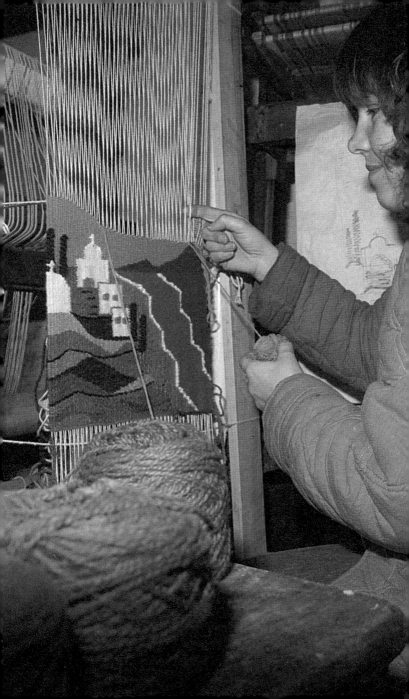

Harris Tweed Association to be made from wool spun and dyed in the Hebrides and handwoven by the islanders of Lewis, Harris, Uist and Barra in their own homes. Most weavers, including the majority of tweed weavers, will send their work to be finished by specialists: the fulling and milling which gives woollen cloth its soft feel and density is difficult to do in small quantities.

Rugs

Making rugs is one of the most popular branches of handweaving. They are usually woven on specially strong floor looms or on a vertical rug loom. To achieve the thickness and heaviness needed for something that has to withstand being walked over, the weft is beaten well down and the warp thread must be very tight for the rug to keep its shape. Many of the patterned weaves can also be used for rugs, and they may also be knotted like carpets.

Braids

Narrow strips of weaving for belts, straps and braids, although they can obviously be woven on a normal loom, are often done on an inkle loom. This is a small frame with a series of pegs round which the braid is woven; the warp is a long continuous loop, so that the length of the braid is limited. Tablet or card weaving is another method of weaving a braid, and requires no loom at all as the warp is looped around some convenient place such as a door handle. Square tablets are punched with four holes through which the warp is threaded, and they are turned between each weft, and patterns are

thus formed. The most primitive of looms, the back-strap loom, can also be used for tablet weaving. The warp is held taut by stretching it between a post (or something similar) and a loop around the waist of the weaver. A weaving method of nomadic tribes, it would be a rare sight in Britain today.

Ikat

'Ikat' is a Malaysian word which has been generally adopted to describe material woven from yarn which has been dip- or tie-dyed different colours prior to weaving. When the yarn is woven the changing colours will form blurred patterns.

The skill in this type of weaving lies as much in the dyeing of the yarn as in the weaving. Ikat is usually woven in cotton or silk, the smoothness of which shows the pattern to its best advantage. The weaver carefully dyes the yarn in sections of colour, planning in advance exactly where they will fall in the weaving.

Knitting

No doubt it would seem strange to a 19th-century knitter that we should regard such work as a beautiful luxury. In the past knitting was an essential part of life – it was a way in which a family could be self-sufficient in clothing, but also it was only through knitting (usually stockings) that many families could earn money for other essentials. Obviously knitting developed mostly in wool-producing areas – the Highlands and Islands of Scotland, in Wales, Yorkshire and the Lake District.

There are also very distinct knitting traditions in coastal and fishing communities: in a pre-mackintosh age a tightly-knit, thick oiled jersey was your best defence against biting sea winds and salt spray. The most famous of these is the Aran sweater from Ireland. Out of the necessity for such work, traditional patterns and colourings of great beauty and skill evolved. That there should be so many regional differences, not only from county to county but also from village to village – even from family to family – is not surprising when one realises that everyone knitted: men, women and children.

It was also a social activity. A description by William Howitt of the Yorkshire Dales in 1840 tells how: 'As soon as it becomes dark, and the usual business of the day is over . . . [they] take their cloaks and lanterns and set out with their knitting to the house of the neighbour . . . The whole troop of neighbours being collected, they sit and knit, sing knitting songs, and tell knitting-stories . . . All this time their knitting goes on with unremitting speed . . .' Imagining this scene it is easy to see how particular patterns would have evolved in a community. Some women knitted almost unceasingly throughout the day, helped by knitting aids. They had knitting sheaths or sticks, which were often beautifully carved and stuck in the waistband to hold one needle. This left one hand free to work the yarn and move stitches to the point of the needle. This way they could also knit while walking about or standing. Sometimes they also had a holder for wool tucked into their skirts.

Fair Isle and Shetland

The traditional Scottish patterns are probably the most elaborate and famous. Fair Isle knitting originated on that island, but it has now been adopted by the whole of Scotland. There is a legend that the multi-coloured patterns were copied from the clothes of Spanish sailors in the Armada (1588) who were wrecked on the island. They have such names as Armada Cross, Star of Life, Sacred Heart and Rose of Sharon.

True traditional Shetland knitting shows off the dark browns, greys and black of the Shetland wool, and it is knitted in geometric motifs which are often similar to Scandinavian patterns. The beautiful fine lace knitting also associated with the Shetlands was developed in the last century at Unst (one of the northernmost islands) when the inhabitants were shown some fine European lace. They then produced their own versions, which were traditionally used for christening shawls. Regional differences in dress are also pinpointed by the knitting of an area, hence the elaborate tops to kilt hose, or the shawls typical of Welsh dress.

Knitting machines

It is very time-consuming to knit clothes by hand, so most of what is termed 'handknitting' today is in fact done on a small machine operated by hand. This allows for the energies and the skills of the craftsman to be concentrated on the colours, patterns and textures, which are often more exciting and adventurous than ever. Some sections will be knitted by hand and the finishing will be individual.

Basket made from buff and brown rods

Making the back to an Orkney chair

Using a burner to melt metal

Tooling leather in a bindery

Bobbin lace making

Traditional patterns, particularly of Fair Isle, Shetland and fishing jerseys, are still produced, though sometimes by mass-manufacture.

Crochet

Crochet is knitting produced with only a single hooked needle. The word derives from the French for hook and the method was developed in 16th-century Europe and became very popular in the 19th century. Although today work is often in wool, the technique is versatile and cotton, linen, and even silk thread can be used. As stitches are worked individually and not in rows (as with normal knitting), the work is more delicate and less restricted in shape. The effects achieved are generally very decorative.

Macramé

Macramé is a recent addition to the crafts practised in Britain. It originated with the Arabs and in Mediterranean countries, where very beautiful and complicated decorative knotting was done. It is also one element in the origins of lace-making. However, British seamen, and to a lesser extent narrowboat people, did while away long hours at sea or on the water producing decoratively knotted belts, bell-pulls and mats – known as 'square-knotting'.

During the Victorian period it was a pastime for ladies to make fringes for mantle shelves, table-mats, runners and anti-macassars. The craft has been widely revived during the last 20 years and new ways of application devised.

Although macramé has always been made with thick string, jute and sisal, more delicate threads are now being used. It can be combined with tapestries, created as wall-hangings, applied to clothes, used for bags, belts, and so on.

Lacemaking

To make even a small section of lace takes many hours, so handmade lacemaking has rarely, if ever, been a way to support a family. Although there were men lacemakers, it was usually the province of women and children, who worked to augment the family income. In the 20th century handmade lace is almost impossibly expensive, but the craft has been kept alive by amateurs since the turn of the century. It was recognized then that handmade lace was far superior to machined lace and this provoked a revival of interest.

There are two ways of making lace: needle lace, which developed from cutwork and drawn-thread work; and bobbin lace, where the thread is twisted and plaited – an evolution from macramé and the decorative knotting of the warp fringes at the end of a section of woven cloth.

Bobbin lace

Bobbin lace is also called 'pillow lace' and 'bone lace' (after the bone bobbins) and it is this type that has always been more popular in England. It was introduced from the Continent in the 17th century by emigrés escaping religious persecution.

It was immediately sought after for trimming fashionable clothes. The lacemakers settled in Devon and in areas of Bedfordshire and Buckinghamshire, establishing these places as centres for lace, a connection which remains to the present day.

The image of the lacemaker has remained unchanged: whenever possible, she sat out of doors to get the maximum amount of light by which to 'twist' and 'cross' the finest linen thread. A pillow of straw-filled hessian or canvas rested on a wooden cradle or 'horse' across the lacemaker's knee. The pattern for the lace (which was usually based on French or Brussels examples) was pricked out on parchment, vellum or stiffened paper, and laid over the pillow to give guidance. Beside her lay thread and a pin cushion. The thread was wound onto bobbins which lay over the edge of the pillow; their weight gave tension to the thread and also enabled the lacemaker to identify each thread as she quickly moved them about. If the lacemaker was forced to work inside or in the evening she would often put a lacemaker's lamp beside her candle; this was a globe of glass which, when filled with water, magnified the precious candlelight.

Bobbins virtually became an art in themselves and the lacemaker took and still takes pride in her collection. Usually turned from wood or bone they might also have been of glass, pewter or ivory. Intricately carved and decorated, they were often inscribed with the owner's name, initials or a saying. For some types of lace it was helpful to have a 'spangle' at the end of the bobbin (a little group of beads wired on, which helped the bobbin to lie flat, thus holding the thread still).

Devon was known for its flounces of lace and the East Midlands for its straight edges and borders. Both declined with the invention of machines which could produce work, though not of the same quality, both quicker and cheaper. Despite patronage from Queen Victoria, whose wedding lace was made of Honiton lace, the numbers of lacemakers dwindled to a very few by the beginning of this century.

Northern Ireland also has a tradition of lacemaking which dates from the mid-19th century when it was encouraged as a form of employment after the ravages of the Potato Famine. Flax has always been grown in Ireland, so the linen thread was easily available, and very fine crochet work in lace patterns is also traditional to this area.

Lacemaking is regaining ground as a hobby and is being more widely taught. Most is still made in the traditional stylised flowers and arabesques. It is now impossible to buy thread of the fineness previously used, so lacemakers are beginning to break new ground, incorporating new types of thread and working on new designs.

Embroidery

Hand embroidery is very time-consuming, but it is also a craft where virtuoso skill can be a source of complete wonderment. The traditions of British embroidery are long, and in a sense, twofold. On the one hand there is the very fine and fashionable work, and on the other the 'folk' embroidery, often making up in vitality what it lacks in finesse. Examples of the first category are the medieval church vestments, Mary Queen of Scots' embroideries with the patterns taken from Renaissance engravings, or 18th-century crewel work hangings richly coloured in imitation of exotic Indian chintzes.

Into the second category fall the embroidered wool pictures worked by sailors during the long hours at sea, showing seascapes or portraits of Royal Navy ships; or the richly embroidered sections on smocks which were once the almost universal dress of the British country dweller. While some smocks were comparatively simple, those from the West of England, Wales and the Midlands often had elaborate cuffs and collars and smocking patterns, particularly on those garments reserved for Sunday best or weddings.

Modern embroidery

The sewing machine, which liberated so many Victorian seamstresses, was also perhaps the beginning of the decline in needlework skills – no longer were embroidery, tucking, cording, appliqué, drawn-thread work, beadwork, and so on, considered essential accomplishments. But modern embroidery has been emancipated in some respects, for it can combine machine- and hand-sewing, with any of the techniques so exquisitely used in the past. Some modern embroiderers work with collage which, although a quite recent term, has its roots in the past: in appliqué on patchwork quilts, beadwork, and even, possibly, in the ornate costumes

Quilting patchwork

of the Cockney Pearly Kings and Queens.

Apart from fine silk and cotton embroidery, there remains the tradition of wool stitched onto canvas (confusingly, sometimes called 'tapestry'). The 'canvas' is a stiff mesh of threads completely covered by wool stitches. A great variety of these stitches has developed throughout Europe, with names such as Florentine or Bargello, Hungarian point, etc.

Much of the finest modern embroidery is done under the patronage of the Church and can be seen on altar cloths, kneelers and vestments, but there has also been a welcome revival in embroidered clothing.

Fabric printing and dyeing

Most fabric today is printed, thousands of metres at a time, on huge rollers. Craftsmen in textiles, however, use other techniques which allow them the freedom to translate their ideas onto the fabric in small runs of material or one-off pieces.

Silk-screen printing

The old method of printing fabric is to use a woodblock, but cutting a pattern on wood is a laborious business and block-printing with lino, rubber and even potatoes is quicker and can be as effective. It is the silk-screen method which has really given the printing process such flexibility, and it is possible to use it on paper, textiles, leather, glass and ceramics. It originated in Japan and has only come into common use during this century. The pattern is blocked out on a panel of tightly-stretched silk, and the dye is then squeezed through the silk, leaving a stencilled effect on the fabric. Often a design will involve half-a-dozen different screens. Although a semi-industrial process, it can be a good vehicle for fine textile design that would never be produced on a larger scale.

Wax resist dyeing

Wax resist dyeing of cloth is a technique that has been used for many centuries, but much modern work is done in the **batik** manner, which comes from Java. The Dutch, whose colony Java was, first appreciated the exquisite work produced there at the end of the 19th century and since then Europeans have decorated cloth in this way.

The design is drawn on in wax, the cloth is dyed and the wax subsequently removed. The process can be repeated many times with layers of colour building up as different areas are waxed over. The characteristic by which batik is recognised is the *craquelure* effect, where the dye has seeped through cracks in the wax. Sometimes these are of a hair's breadth, and often the material is deliberately crumpled up to accentuate the cracks.

Tie dyeing

Tie dyeing is another technique from the East – particularly good examples come from Rajasthan in India. This involves tying up tiny bunches of the cloth so that when it is dipped into the dye these sections remain uncoloured. Sadly, in the countries of origin these hand techniques are often imitated by large-scale printing, whereas in their country of adoption their possibilities are now being fully explored.

As dyes and pigments have developed, so have new ways of using them. Sometimes they are sprayed on with an air-brush, a simple device which will spray a fine mist of colour, avoiding hard lines and edges. Many craftsmen will also paint the dye directly onto the fabric, usually silk or cotton. This can produce a richness and subtlety not found in more conventionally printed or dyed fabrics.

See also **ikat weaving** (p.52).

Quilting, patchwork and appliqué

Necessity is the mother of invention, and the patchwork quilt is an excellent example of this dictum. In the days when more value was placed on a scrap of fabric, particularly if it was printed or brightly coloured, nothing was wasted when lots of small pieces were joined together. Similarly, worn or torn pieces of material could be re-used if an appliqué was superimposed on top of the hole. All these otherwise useless bits and pieces could be made into a warm bedcovering if two layers were infilled with wool. Near importing or manufacturing centres such as Lancashire or Durham cotton or linen were often used instead. The lines of quilting stitchery held the filling in place. These rather mundane objects became works of

great beauty, and by the 19th century it is likely that some quilts were made with fabrics bought specially for the purpose.

Patchwork is usually in geometric shapes, which are easy to stitch together: diamonds, squares, hexagons, triangles and stripes. By using appliqué, figurative sections could be added – flowers, plants, animals, even historical scenes. There was no restraint on the quilting stitches, and they often formed beautiful swirling motifs, such as arabesques, rosettes and feather patterns. In some areas of Britain, such as Durham, Ayrshire and Carmarthenshire, it was popular to make quilts without patches or appliqué but to concentrate on the quilting stitches.

Modern techniques

Craftsmen today make full use of all these techniques, but have greatly widened their application. Patchwork is often made of fabric that has been carefully chosen for texture and colour, possibly specially dyed to exactly the right shade. The seams and quilting are sometimes machine stitched. Bedcoverings are still a perfect vehicle for the craft, but often the pieces are so subtle that they are better seen as wall-hangings.

The warmth of quilting has been well adapted to clothing, a revival of a style of dress common in both the Middle Ages and Elizabethan period. Modern quilters have also explored the three-dimensional quality of the technique, and sometimes accentuated it by spray-dyeing or painting dye directly onto the fabric.

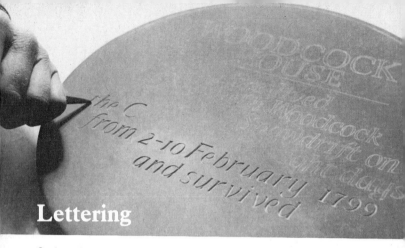

Lettering

Carving a plaque of Welsh slate

Letters can be intrinsically beautiful, but this is often not appreciated until the work of a calligrapher or letter cutter is studied. Like so many crafts this is one that has been revitalized in the 20th century, and the need for lettering will never cease. Fine lettering has a range of uses, from memorials in wood and stone and commemorative silver, to ceramics or glass, scrolls and certificates and lettering for reproduction on book jackets and letterheads.

The craftsman considers what message the letters are to convey. This guides him on the form that the lettering will take: not only the letters themselves, but how they are arranged in the space. Usually a calligrapher specializes either in writing or in letter cutting, but some can work in many media.

Calligraphy was raised to an art by medieval monks working on illuminated manuscripts, which in a pre-printing age were the only way that a text could be circulated. Their materials – vellum, hand-made ink, goose-quill pen – are those that craftsmen today find most exciting to work with. They say that a quill pen on vellum can produce effects never attainable with paper and fountain pen.

Calligraphers will usually prepare their own pens and inks – the goose quills are softened in water, trimmed to the right shape and then hardened by heating, often by pressing them in hot sand; the inks can be mixed to exactly the right consistency. Work on the expensive calfskin vellum (a skin which has been stretched and scraped in a particular way) and handmade papers is often gilded. This is done by applying pure gold leaf of infinitesimal thinness to gesso, a special composition made mainly of plaster and white lead. The gold leaf is then burnished to a brilliant shine by rubbing it with a highly polished hardstone.

Whether the lettering is chiselled out of slate or oak, painted or drawn, mistakes are difficult, if not impossible, to correct, and it is the skill of the letterer that allows him to form the shape and sweeps with confidence, producing work which has the hallmark of a craftsman.

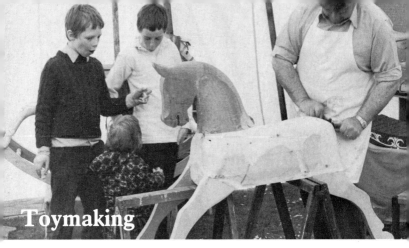

Making a traditional rocking horse

Toymaking

There is a strong element of nostalgia in craftsman-made toys, but this is not surprising, given the plastic revolution in toymaking in the last 20 years. Toys have been rendered virtually unbreakable, brilliantly coloured and common to children all over the British Isles – if not Europe and America as well.

Archeological finds dating from antiquity show that children's tastes have altered little: dolls and animals, wheeled toys which developed from horse and cart to racing cars, and games. By the 19th century a nursery culture was developing and toys and games greatly increased in range and variety: jigsaws (first called 'dissected pictures'), clockwork toys and many board games. Novelty and innovation are always a passion with children, hence the popularity of the 19th-century steam engine and the 20th-century spacecraft.

There have long been, and still are, toys which are really for adults. 'Baby houses', as they were called, were a popular amusement for adults in the 18th century: immaculately recreated households with real silver and fashionable furniture created by cabinet makers. By the end of the century the fashion passed and they were relegated to children's toys, but once again there are now many craftsmen making models of period furniture and furnishings for serious doll's-house collectors. Scale models of cars and trains are equally unsuitable for children, but are collected by adults. Puppet theatres (Punch arrived in England from Italy as early as 1666) and rocking horses are both toys whose popularity has waned little since the 18th century.

The craftsman toymaker today has much in common with the 'toyman' of the 18th century, producing small ranges or one-off originals of beautifully made toys, and as before the clients are not all children. Wood is once more the prime material, and the inspiration is usually from the past. There is, however, a wit present in them which is not so common in mass-manufactured toys.

Where to See & Buy Crafts
A Regional Guide

Stoneware boxes

This section lists workshops, museums, craft centres, galleries and shops where craft work, ancient as well as modern, can be seen and bought and, often, commissioned.

They are grouped by regions and listed alphabetically under village or town. Inevitably some areas have more entries listed than others. For instance, the South West appears notably more craft-conscious than other regions.

Apart from museums, opening times are not given, as they may well vary according to circumstances. If you are travelling from a distance it is obviously well worthwhile to check the opening times before you set out. Remember, too, that in remoter areas of Britain places are often open only in summer, or have much shorter hours during winter.

Craftsmen can normally be seen at work at these workshops, forges and potteries – this is one of the reasons for their being included. However, it is worth remembering that working craftsmen are not 'exhibits' and must earn their living by their craft. Fascinating though it may be for the visitor, the craftsmen may not have time to stop, talk and explain his work at length. You enter their place of work at their discretion. Further, intricate work such as jewellery or bookbinding is often unsuitable for showing to large groups, so for crafts such as these the best place to see finished work is often in a gallery or shop.

London and the South East

Kent, Sussex, Surrey and Greater London

Although London now dominates this area, the South East does have its own characteristics. Much of the Weald of Kent was thickly forested, mainly with oak, and the traditional local crafts were based on wood, as well as iron, which used wood as fuel for smelting. While there is no single, distinctive, widespread craft typical to the region, there are a number which are traditional, using the wool, clay and other materials which abound in this fertile corner of England.

As with any capital city, London is the centre for artistic activity. While relatively few craftsmen work in the city, it is here that some of the best contemporary work can be seen. Apart from the major publicly-funded galleries and museums, there are a number of lively private galleries and craft markets.

Brighton
Barclaycraft Craft Gallery
7 East Street, Brighton, East Sussex. Tel Brighton 21694
Sells contemporary crafts, individually made by British studio craftsmen, particularly ceramics, gold and silver jewellery, glass and wood. Separate gallery with regular one-man and group exhibitions.

Chichester
Hands
150 St Pancras, Chichester, West Sussex. Tel Chichester 787645
Craft gallery selling high quality work: glass, ceramics, weaving, ironwork, wood, inexpensive jewellery, crochet and prints.

Ditchling
The Craftsman Gallery & *Jill Pryke, Potter*
8 High Street, Ditchling, East Sussex. Tel Hassocks 5246
The gallery shows a wide range of crafts made in Sussex (metalwork, silver, jewellery, batik, weaving, wood turning and engraving, glass, corn dollies and pottery). Jill Pryke's pottery shares the premises, where she produces a range of green glazed earthenware. Index of Sussex craftsmen and information section.

East Grinstead
David Hensel
1 Medway Drive, East Grinstead, West Sussex. Tel East Grinstead 27578
Jeweller and silversmith producing small-scale sculpture incorporating woods, ivory, stones, mother of pearl, etc.

Godalming
The Wharf Pottery
55 St John Street, Farncombe, Godalming, Surrey. Tel Godalming 4097
Mary Wondrausch works in slip-trailed and sgraffito earthenware and specializes in commemorative ware, egg stands, harvest jugs, owl jugs and cheese platters in the tradition of English folk pottery.

Henfield
Henfield Woodcraft
Harwoods Farm, West End Lane, Henfield, West Sussex. Tel Henfield 492820
Peter Spear is a specialist turner of salad bowls and platters, all in English hardwoods which he buys and saws in Sussex. Telephone to arrange visit.

Herstmonceux
Thomas Smith
(Herstmonceux)
Gardener Street, Herstmonceux, nr Hailsham, East Sussex. Tel Herstmonceux 832137
Shop selling the Sussex trug baskets first made by this company in the 19th c.

Horsham
Horsham Museum
9 The Causeway, Horsham, West Sussex. Tue-Fri 1-5, Sat 10-5
Domestic and rural life museum with saddler's shop, blacksmith's forge and wheelwright.

London
Amalgam
3 Barnes High Street, London SW13. Tel (01) 878 1279
Gallery showing the work of mainly London-based artist craftsmen: ceramics, blown glass, jewellery and prints.

Argenta Gallery
82 Fulham Road, London SW3. Tel (01) 584 3119
Gallery showing the work of 25 to 30 contemporary jewellers, each piece individually made. Periodic special exhibitions.

Aspects
3-5 Whitfield Street, London W1. Tel (01) 580 7563
A new gallery specializing in modern experimental jewellery, mainly in non-precious materials.

Basilisk Press
32 England's Lane, London
NW3. Tel (01) 722 2142
The bookshop sells books
from British private presses
and other fine limited
editions. Also calligraphy,
hand-marbled papers and
wood engravings.

Briglin Pottery
23 Crawford Street, London
W1. Tel (01) 935 0605
Brigitta Appleby's pottery,
established in 1948. With
four assistants she
specializes in red
earthenware decorated with
wax-resist and on-glaze
brushwork.

British Crafts Centre
43 Earlham Street, London
WC2. Tel (01) 836 6993
The headquarters of the
national association for
contemporary crafts.
Constantly changing
exhibitions of work by the
finest British craftsmen.
Also pieces for sale.

Camden Lock
Chalk Farm Road, London
NW1
Workshops in group of
buildings beside the
Regent's Canal. Craftsmen
include: potter, stained
glass maker, jewellers,
musical instrument maker,
leatherworker, glass
engraver, weaver,
handpainted silk, furniture
makers and embroiderer.
Craft stalls at weekends.

Casson Gallery
73 Marylebone High Street,
London W1. Tel (01) 487
5080
Gallery selling work by
Britain's foremost artist
craftsmen: porcelain and
stoneware, jewellery, studio
glass and turned and carved
wood.

Crafts Council Gallery
12 Waterloo Place, Lower
Regent Street, London
SW1. Tel (01) 930 4811
Changing exhibitions of
work by leading innovative
craftsmen. Index of
craftsmen working in all
media illustrated by slides

of their work (can be viewed
by appointment with the
Librarian). Each craftsman
has met the standards
imposed by the Crafts
Council panel.

Craftsmen Potters Shop
William Blake House,
Marshall Street, London
W1. Tel (01) 437 7605
Sells and exhibits studio
pottery by members of the
Craftsmen Potters
Association.

Joël Degen
42 Dinerman Court, 38/40
Boundary Road, London
NW8. Tel (01) 624 7213
Jewellery workshop
producing a wide range in
titanium, stainless steel,
aluminium, plastics, glass,
terylene and polyester
thread, also work in more
traditional gold, silver,
precious and semi-precious
stones. Workshop can be
visited by appointment.

Electrum Gallery
21 South Molton Street,
London W1. Tel (01) 629
6325
Gallery which shows and
sells the work of leading
contemporary jewellers.

Sam Herman
7 Chelsea Wharf, 15 Lots
Road, London SW10. Tel
(01) 352 4080
One of the longest
established of the studio
glassmakers working in
Britain. Workshop can be
visited by appointment.

Kingsgate Workshops
110-116 Kingsgate Road,
London NW6. Tel (01) 328
7878
35 workshops with crafts
including woven textiles,
handpainted and quilted
clothes, textile painting and
printing, puppet making
and furniture making in
pine, quality hardwoods,
bamboo and cane. Also
seven potters and ceramists
working in majolica,
porcelain and stoneware,
and handpainted tiles.

*London Glassblowing
Workshop and Gallery*
109 Rotherhithe Street,
London SE16. Tel (01) 237
0394
Three glassblowers work
with free-blown glass, each
piece individually coloured
and handformed.

Bronson Shaw
The Granary,
61 St Marychurch Street,
London SE16.
Tel (01) 994 3212
Craftsmen in stained glass;
stained glass windows and
Tiffany-style lamps made to
order. Workshop not open
to the public.

The Glasshouse
65 Long Acre, London
WC2. Tel (01) 836 9785
Six glassblowers share
workshop. Individual pieces
are displayed in the gallery,
behind which is the furnace
where the hot glass is
worked.

*The Handweavers Studio &
Gallery*
29 Haroldstone Road,
London E17. Tel (01) 521
2281
Shop sells rugs, bedspreads,
blankets, scarves, lengths of
fabric and wall-hangings.
Courses in weaving are run
here and the students can
sometimes be seen at work.

Victoria and Albert Museum
Cromwell Road, London
SW7. Tel (01) 589 6371.
Mon-Thur, Sat 10-6,
Sun 2-5
The most important
collection of decorative art
in the country, with
exceptional examples of
work in all media.
Craft Shop V&A (Tel (01)
589 5070) sells a selection of
high quality work.

THAMES VALLEY & SOUTH

Thames Valley and South

Berkshire, Buckinghamshire, Hampshire, Oxfordshire and the Isle of Wight

There tend to be fewer well-defined regional traditions and crafts in such a central and well-populated area of Britain. However, the old rural crafts have been as much part of this area's history as any other.

The most famous of these is probably the chair making in the Chiltern hills. Using the wood from the plantations of tall, straight beech trees, the 'chair bodgers' would work in the open with a simple pole lathe turning the green wood into legs, spars and stretchers for chairs. These sections were then taken to towns and villages such as High Wycombe, Stokenchurch and Penn, where the chair makers completed the chairs. These country-made chairs, which usually ignored the latest fashions of shape and ornament, are often known as Windsor chairs.

Peasmarsh
Frank Smith
Old Winders House, Peasmarsh, near Rye, East Sussex. Tel Peasmarsh 284
Potter producing handthrown stoneware, porcelain, and garden pots.

Pevensey
Glynleigh Studio
Peelings Lane, Pevensey, East Sussex. Tel Eastbourne 763456
Metalworkers in copper, brass, bronze, etc. They also make the traditional Sussex crook.

Rye
Rye Pottery
Ferry Road, Rye, East Sussex. Tel Rye 3363
In a town with a long tradition of potters, John and Walter Cole produce ranges of handmade and handpainted majolica and stoneware.

Sandwich
Sally Gordon Boyd, Homeweaves
53 New Street, Sandwich, Kent. Tel Sandwich 617272
Specializing in handwoven and handknitted items, all in pure wool.

Shere
Shere Potter
The Studio, Lower Street, Shere, nr Guildford, Surrey. Tel Shere 2626
Chris Otway's pottery, where he makes functional domestic stoneware.

Sittingbourne
Old Mill Tonge
Tonge, Sittingbourne, Kent. Tel Sittingbourne 78300
Craft centre showing the work of about 60 local craftsmen. Occasional craft demonstrations.

Strood
Silvercraft
10 North Street, Strood, Kent. Tel Medway 724761
Shop selling the work of Geoff Buchan, jeweller and silversmith.

Aldermaston
Aldermaston Pottery
Aldermaston, Berkshire. Tel Woolhampton 3359
Alan Caiger-Smith produces a wide range of tableware, decorative pieces and tiles. Mainly tin-glaze earthenware with brush-painted decoration. Showroom with work for sale. The Pottery itself can sometimes be visited.

Andover
Foxcotte Tower Galleries
Foxcotte Lane, Charlton, nr Andover, Hampshire. Tel Andover 53056
Craft gallery specializing in pottery and wood turning, carving and sculpture. Occasional exhibitions.

Aylesbury
Ivor Newton & Son
Aston Road, Haddenham, Aylesbury, Buckinghamshire. Tel Aylesbury 291461
Cabinet makers, wood-carvers and joiners. Also antique restoration.

Beaconsfield
Lake, Muckley & Co.
1 Wycombe End, Beaconsfield, Buckinghamshire. Tel Beaconsfield 3632
Metalworkers producing wrought ironwork gates, grilles, lamps, etc.

Bicester
Chesterton Pottery
Chesterton, nr Bicester, Oxfordshire. Tel Bicester 41455
Pottery workshop where Tony Smythe produces handthrown earthenware with slip decoration.

Bishops Waltham
The Old Granary Art and Craft Centre
Bank Street, Bishops Waltham, Hampshire. Tel Bishops Waltham 4700
Craft shop and art gallery. Also workshops including: potter, textile designer, model coachmaker, gold-smith, leatherworker, screen printers, violin maker, ceramist and toymaker.

Bracknell
South Hill Park Arts Centre
Bracknell, Berkshire. Tel
Bracknell 27272
Workshops include: Karen
Ford, weaver of silk and
jeweller; Philippa Cronin,
potter in porcelain and
stoneware, some pieces cast
with inlaid decoration;
Valerie Mead, jeweller and
silversmith; Peter Child,
jeweller using gold, silver,
nickel-silver and faceted
stones. The *Shop at the Park*
sells the work of these
craftsmen and also an
extensive range of ceramics,
jewellery, textiles, toys and
cards. Special displays each
month.

Clanfield
Crowdys Wood Products
The Old Bakery, Clanfield,
nr Oxford. Tel Clanfield 216
Cabinet makers, wood
turners and furniture
designers, producing garden
furniture, lamps, tableware,
spinning wheels. The *Craft
Shop* also sells pottery,
textiles, leatherwork, etc.

Cropredy
Prescote Gallery
Cropredy, nr Banbury,
Oxfordshire. Tel Banbury
75660
Work by designer craftsmen
from all over Britain:
textiles, ceramics, glass,
wood, toys and fine
furniture.

Deddington
*Michael and Heather
Ackland*
Coniston House, New
Street, Deddington, nr
Oxford. Tel Deddington
38241
Jewellers working in gold
and silver, also making
small silver pieces and wood
and silver boxes. Work
shown in gallery, also
selected work by other
craftsmen: pottery,
woodwork, etc.

Froxfield
Edward Barnsley Partnership
Cockshott Lane, Froxfield,
nr Petersfield, Hampshire.
Tel Hawkley 233
Edward Barnsley is the son
of Sydney Barnsley, the
architect, furniture designer
and co-founder the
Cotswold school of furniture
designers and craftsmen at
the turn of the century: an
important figure in the craft
revival. Three senior
craftsmen and three
apprentices work at the
Edward Barnsley
Partnership making
wooden furniture in this
tradition.

Great Missenden
Bucks Bobbins
Woodside, Greenlands
Lane, Prestwood, Great
Missenden,
Buckinghamshire. Tel
Great Missenden 5283
Telephone to make an
appointment to see
handmade lace bobbins and
pillows and other
lacemaking equipment
made in one of the
traditional lacemaking
areas.

Henley-on-Thames
Aston Pottery
Aston Farm House,
Remenham Lane, Henley-
on-Thames, Oxfordshire.
Tel Henley 2603
A joint workshop
producing domestic ware,
ceramic sculpture in
stoneware and porcelain,
and small bronze
sculptures.

High Wycombe
*Wycombe Chair and Local
History Museum*
Castle Hill, High
Wycombe,
Buckinghamshire. Tel High
Wycombe 23879. Mon-Sat
10-1, 2-5 (not Weds)
Chair collection
concentrates on locally-
made Windsor type. Also
exhibition of woodworking
tools and equipment and
other local work, including
Buckinghamshire lace.

Hook Norton
Hook Norton Pottery
East End Farmhouse, Hook
Norton, nr Banbury,
Oxfordshire. Tel Hook
Norton 737414
A large range of domestic
stoneware as well as
individual pieces, mostly
large bowls and jars.

Isle of Wight
Chessell Pottery
Chessell, nr Yarmouth. Tel
I.o.W. 78248
Pottery with large output of
decorative handmade
porcelain based on natural
forms, mainly with a marine
theme.

Island Glass
London House, Queens
Road, Freshwater. Tel
I.o.W. 753473
Michael Rayner makes a
range of table and
decorative glassware, and
glass clocks, in his studio.
Large showroom also sells
silver and glass jewellery.

*Isle of Wight Country Craft
Workshops*
Arreton Manor Farm,
Arreton. Tel I.o.W. 528353
12 workshops which are let
to craftsmen on a yearly
basis. Therefore there is a
changing population of
craftworkers, who all sell
directly to the public.

Isle of Wight Glass
Old Park, St Lawrence,
Ventnor. Tel I.o.W. 853526
Team of glassmakers
handmaking a range of
coloured glass.

Milton Keynes
Great Linford Arts Centre
The Manor, Great Linford
Village, Milton Keynes,
Buckinghamshire. Tel
Milton Keynes 663966
There are three craftsmen in
residence in this new Arts
Centre: Colin Thornbury
(Workshop 3, The Alms-
houses, Tel M. K. 662828),
potter in porcelain and
stoneware using crystalline
and metallic glazes; W. S.
Wortley (4 Pritchard
Almshouse Buildings, Tel

M. K. 605919), hand engraver mostly working on gold and silver, telephone for appointment to visit; Clare Layton (Workshop 4, Almshouse 5, Tel M.K. 605918), jeweller working mainly in gold and specializing in repoussé decoration. Exhibitions in the Manor House. Courses and classes are held.

Minstead
Will Selwood Gallery
Furzey Gardens, Minstead, nr Lyndhurst, Hampshire. Tel Cadnam 2464
Gallery showing the work of local craftsmen, some amateur: jewellery, pottery, woodwork, leather, glass, furniture, etc.

Oxford
Oxford Gallery
23 High Street, Oxford. Tel Oxford 42731
Gallery which shows high quality work of British and foreign artists and craftsmen, especially ceramics and jewellery. Regular exhibitions.

Portsmouth
City Museum and Art Gallery
Museum Road, Old Portsmouth, Hampshire. Tel Portsmouth 827261. Daily 10.30-5.30
Museum which, in addition to its historical collection of the decorative arts, displays work by modern craftsmen.

Reading
George Frost Basket Maker
5 Pursers Farm, Basingstoke Road, Spencers Wood, Reading, Berkshire. Tel Reading 882267
Using willow and cane, George Frost makes baskets and cane furniture.

Museum of English Rural Life
Whiteknights, University of Reading, Berkshire. Tel Reading 85123. Tue-Fri 10-4.30, Sat 10-1, 2-4.30
Museum of the history of English country life, agriculture, and crafts.

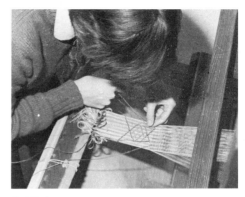

An inkle loom

Selborne
Peter Ingram
Limes End Yard, High Street, Selborne, nr Alton, Hampshire
Coachbuilder and painter, restorer and decorator of gypsy caravans. Also a small Romany Folklore Museum.

Southampton
Overstone Pottery
260 Brook Lane, Sarisbury, Southampton. Tel Locks Heath 84474
Pottery which sells its range of decorated tin-glazed earthenware: mugs, jugs, coffee sets, bowls, etc. Workshop not open to the public.

Southampton Art Gallery
Civic Centre, Commercial Road, Southampton. Tel Southampton 23855 ext 759
The Gallery has made a collection of the work of modern British potters. The *Museum Shop* sells the work of mainly Southern potters.

Speen
Joyce Coleman
Spinning Wheel Cottage, Speen, nr Aylesbury, Buckinghamshire. Tel Hampden Row 303
Handloom weaver and spinner working in wool, cotton, linen and silk, making blankets, cot blankets, cushions, etc.

Upton
Barbara Price
Springside Cottage, Stream Road, Upton, nr Didcot, Oxfordshire. Tel Blewbury 850526
Enameller, principally making pictures in transparent enamel on copper. Also works in silver and makes millefiori beads.

Wallingford
Haddon Rockers
Station Road Industrial Estate, Wallingford, Oxfordshire. Tel Wallingford 36165
Makers and restorers of rocking horses.

West Meon
Meon Pottery
Church Lane, West Meon, nr Petersfield, Hampshire. Tel West Meon 434
Nigel Wood specializes in terracotta garden pots in traditional local shapes with Hampshire clay, also makes stoneware and porcelain.

Winterbourne
Bridge Pottery
Winterbourne, nr Newbury, Berkshire. Tel Chieveley 312
David Tipler's pottery, which sells domestic stoneware and some porcelain and lustre-glazed items.

East Anglia

Cambridgeshire, Essex, Norfolk and Suffolk

This is one of the least populated parts of England, much of it consisting of wide open, flat, arable land. The early wealth of East Anglia was based on wool, and many Suffolk and Norfolk towns and villages have a large church or building dating from medieval times. East Anglia eventually lost its supremacy in the wool trade, but the tradition of fine weaving remained, notably the Norfolk shawls.

The fenlands, the wide river estuaries and the Norfolk Broads are excellent for rushes and osier, so rushwork, basketry and thatching are all traditional crafts practised here. Straw, too, is available in abundance and is put to good use by local craftsmen.

Acle
Julie Woods Pottery
The Street, Acle, nr Norwich, Norfolk
Shop selling work by Julie Woods and other local potters, also some corn dollies and jewellery.

Aldringham
Aldringham Craft Market
nr Leiston, Suffolk. Tel Leiston 830397
Set in several buildings around a garden. Displays various crafts but specializes in ceramics by well-known craftsmen potters, and the work of the owner, Muriel Wright. Jewellery, turned and carved wood and glass also sold.

Boxford
Falcon House Gallery
Swan Street, Boxford, Suffolk. Tel Boxford 210138
Permanent stock and special exhibitions of individually made one-off pieces by artist-craftsmen: concentrates on ceramics but also has studio glass, jewellery and stitch and fibre work.

Bury St Edmunds
The Rake Factory
Station Yard, Little Welnetham, Bury St Edmunds, Suffolk. Tel Bury St Edmunds 828630
75-year-old factory where a range of traditional wooden tools, such as scythe snathes (handles) and kitchen articles are made. Most of the wood comes from a nearby 500-year-old coppice.

Cambridge
Cambridge and County Folk Museum
2 & 3 Castle Street, Cambridge. Tel Cambridge 355159. Tue-Fri 10.30-5, Sat 10.30-1, Sun 2.30-4.30. Bank Hol Mon 2-5
Domestic life and crafts from 17th c. to present. Also nursery furniture and toys.

Primavera
10 King's Parade, Cambridge. Tel Cambridge 357708
One of the oldest established craft shops, particularly known for its selection of ceramics, but also glass, jewellery, weaving, etc.

Textile Studio
3 Free School Lane, Cambridge. Tel Cambridge 313583
Shop sells textiles in natural fabric, including handwoven tweed. Gallery above has exhibitions of textile craftsmen.

Colchester
Holy Trinity Church
Trinity Street, Colchester, Essex. Tel Colchester 77475. Mon-Sat, 10-1, 2-5; Oct-Mar closes at 4 on Sat
Redundant church now a museum of country crafts.

Coltishall
Country and Cottage Crafts
Wroxham Road, Coltishall, nr Norwich, Norfolk. Tel Norwich 737549
Shows and sells the work of local craftsmen: furniture, pottery, turned wood, enamel, leatherwork, corn dollies, macramé, glass, etc.

Ely
The Stained Glass Museum
North Triforium, Ely Cathedral, Ely, Cambridgeshire. Tel Ely 5103. Mar-Oct, Mon-Sat 11-4, Sun 12-3
Display of stained glass from the 14th c. to the present. Models of a modern workshop.

Erpingham
Alby Crafts
Cromer Road, Erpingham, Norfolk. Tel Cromer 761590
In a restored group of farmbuildings, there is a large gallery selling the work of 200 craftsmen from all over Britain. 10 studio workshops offer the work of the following: furniture/harp maker, woodcarver, embroiderer, silversmith, signwriter, potter. Also handmade furniture, painted silk clothes and hangings, and leaded lights. Summer exhibitions (gallery closed in winter). Courses in spinning and weaving.

Great Yarmouth
Old Merchants House
Row 117, Great Yarmouth,
Norfolk. Tel Great
Yarmouth 57900. Apr-Sep,
Mon-Fri 9.30-6.30. Closed
May Day hol
Early-17th-c. house
containing collection of
domestic ironwork from
17th to 19th c.

Haddenham
Farmland Museum
50 High Street,
Haddenham,
Cambridgeshire. Tel Ely
740381. Open 1st Sun in
every month, 2-dusk.
Exhibition of rural crafts
and agricultural bygones.

Harlow
Parndon Mill
off Elizabeth Way, Harlow,
Essex.
Large old mill converted
into 14 craft studios
including those of a wood
turner, jeweller, potter,
cabinet maker.

Langham
Langham Glasshouse
The Long Barn, Langham,
nr Holt, Norfolk. Tel
Binham 511.
Two glassworkers can be
seen blowing and
manipulating the hot glass
to produce animal figures,
vases etc.

Lavenham
Lavenham Guildhall
Market Square, Lavenham,
Suffolk. Daily Mar-end
Nov, 10.30-12.30, 2-5.30
The beautiful 16th-c.
Guildhall was the centre of
the wool trade. Exhibition
of wool manufacture and
coopering.

Meridian
48 High Street, Lavenham,
Suffolk. Tel Lavenham
247923
Craft shop with emphasis on
textiles: patchwork,
appliqué, silk-screened
fabrics made up into
cushions, quilts and
pictures. Also other crafts
such as studio pottery.

Maldon
Oakwood Arts Centre
Friars Walk, Maldon,
Essex. Tel Maldon 56503
Eight craft workshops
attached to the Arts Centre:
furniture maker, spinner
and weaver, jeweller, potter
and needleworker, where
work can be seen in
progress and bought.
Monthly craft market with
demonstrations and craft
classes.

Norwich
Black Horse Craft Centre
10b Wensum Street,
Norwich, Norfolk. Tel
Norwich 612428
Work by leading artists and
craftsmen: a full range of
ceramics, turned wood, toys
and puzzles, studio glass,
embroideries and jewellery.

*Bridewell Museum of Local
Industries*
Bridewell Alley, Norwich.
Tel Norwich 611277 ext
290. Mon-Sat 10-5
Museum covering life and
work of Norwich people
from 18th-20th c. Local
crafts exhibited include
weaving and shoemaking.

Castle Museum Craft Shop
Norwich, Norfolk. Tel
Norwich 611277
Shows and sells work by
exhibiting members of the
Norfolk Contemporary
Crafts Society: ceramics,
glass, wood, toys and
textiles. Index of East
Anglian craftsmen.
Occasional craft
demonstrations.

Oakington
Mark Bury's Workshop
53 Longstanton Road,
Oakington,
Cambridgeshire. Tel Histon
2401
Produces lettering and
pictorial glass engraving,
lettering in stone, wood and
perspex, also heraldic
carving and calligraphy.
Workshop can be visited by
appointment.

Quendon
Quendon Pottery and Crafts
Cambridge Road, Quendon,
nr Saffron Walden, Essex.
Tel Rickling 439
Stoneware pottery made on
the premises by Russ
Smith. Other potters' work
also on display, with
Norfolk baskets, weaving,
patchwork, turned wood
and metalwork.

Snape
Snape Craft Centre
Snape Maltings, Snape
Bridge, nr Saxmundham,
Suffolk. Tel Snape 305
Gallery exhibits crafts and
prints. Craft shop
specializes in East Anglian
work. Several workshops on
the site include a furniture
maker, blacksmith and
piano maker/restorer.

Snettisham
Snettisham Studio
1 Lynn Road, Snettisham,
nr King's Lynn, Norfolk.
Tel Dersingham 41167
Carole Grace is a
handspinner and weaver
using local fleeces dyed with
plants from the surrounding
countryside. Shop sells local
pottery, terracotta, wooden
toys, basketry and corn
dollies, also weavers'
supplies.

Stowmarket
Museum of East Anglian Life
Stowmarket, Suffolk. Tel
Stowmarket 2229. Apr-Oct,
Mon-Sat 11-5, Sun 2-5
Reconstructed buildings
and exhibits relating to the
agriculture, crafts and life of
the area.

Stradbroke
*Robin & Jenny Welch
Pottery*
Stradbroke, Eye, Suffolk.
Tel Stradbroke 416
A large range of domestic
stoneware is made here; the
smaller pieces mould-made,
the large thrown. Also
individual pots and
sculpture by the Welches on
sale in the gallery. Pottery
lessons and demonstrations.

Thaxted
Glendale Forge
Monk Street, Thaxted,
Essex. Tel Thaxted 830466
Forge and showroom which
shows a range of wrought
ironwork and standard
items such as candlesticks,
gates, lanterns, fire-baskets,
etc. Blacksmithing tools also
made.

Wells-next-the-Sea
Bygones at Holkham
Holkham Park, Wells-next-
the-Sea, Norfolk. Tel
Fakenham 710806. End
May-end Sep, Mon-Thur
11-5, Sun 2-5
Display in the stables of
Holkham Hall (fine
Palladian house, open to the
public) which includes
display of craft tools. Craft
demonstrations on certain
days. Also Pottery within
the Park.

The Sackhouse Craft Gallery
The Wells Centre, Staithe
Street, Wells, Norfolk. Tel.
Fakenham 710130
Attached to Arts Centre,
gallery shows regular
exhibitions by East Anglian
craftsmen as well as quality
work from outside the
region. Stocks basketry,
toys, pottery, glass,
woodturning etc.
Programme of
demonstrations planned.

Willingham
Den Young
63 Earith Road,
Willingham,
Cambridgeshire. Tel
Willingham 60015
Craftsman making
miniature furniture and
doll's houses for collectors,
scaled 1 foot to 1 inch.

Witchford
Fenweave
37 Main Street, Witchford,
nr Ely, Cambridgeshire. Tel
Ely 2150
Mr and Mrs Allen produce
woven cotton, linen and
wool on old power looms
dating back 50 years.

The South West

Avon, Devon, Dorset, Cornwall, Somerset and Wiltshire

The potter Bernard Leach established his
pottery at St Ives, Cornwall, in 1920. He was
the first 'studio potter' in Britain and since
then the South West has become increasingly
the area of Britain most closely associated with
contemporary crafts, particularly pottery.
There are workable clays in every county in
England, but the clays of Devon and Cornwall
are especially good and varied and there is a
strong tradition of country pottery. Few
potters now prepare their own clay from
scratch, but there is an undeniable attraction
for craftsmen in being close to the source of
their materials. As a popular holiday area, it
also makes commercial sense for craftworkers
to base themselves here.

Sedgmoor in Somerset, also known as the
'Somerset levels', is the most famous willow-
growing area in Britain. It provides material
not only for local basket-makers, but for
craftsmen all over the country. Another craft
for which the area is famous is lacemaking. It is
centred around Honiton and Beer, in Devon,
because it was here that the 17th-century
refugees from the Continent, who introduced
the art to Britain, settled.

Barnstaple
*The Craft Market and
Workshop*
Church Lane, Barnstaple,
North Devon. Tel
Barnstaple 75171
Several craftworkers have
their workshops here,
including a potter, wood-
turner, spinner and weaver,
leatherworker and printer.

Bath
Bath Crafts and Bath Pottery
Broad Street Place, Bath,
Avon. Tel Bath 62192
Combined craft shop and
workshops. The workshops
house two potters whose
work includes thrown and

decorated stoneware,
slipware, garden pots and
silk screens on ceramics.
Also a jeweller specializing
in silver and titanium
coloured by electrolysis.

*The Crafts Study Centre,
Holburne of Menstrie
Museum*
Great Pulteney Street, Bath,
Avon. Tel Bath 66669 Mon-
Sat 11-5, Sun 2.30-6
Part of the University of
Bath, the Centre has a
collection of work by
leading 20th-c. artist-
craftsmen, which can be
seen in the display gallery.
Also study facilities.

Walcot Pottery and Leather Workshops
87 and 100 Walcot Street, Bath, Avon. Tel Bath 64789
Work of four potters who share a workshop, ranging from table and kitchenware and gardening pots of all kinds, to decorative individual pieces. Bags and belts hand-stitched in fine leather also on sale. Workshop is not open to the public.

Wellow Crafts
Kingsmead Square, Bath, Avon. Tel Bath 64358
Centre for traditional crafts where the work of 180 local craftsmen can be seen. About 30 different crafts are shown: pottery, glass, Dorset buttons, basket and rush work, jewellery, hand-painted toys, rocking horses, patchwork, appliqué, handspun and handwoven articles, etc. Daily demonstrations of crafts.

Beaminster

John Makepeace Furniture Workshops
Parnham House, Beaminster, Dorset. Tel Beaminster 862204.
Workshop & House, Apr-Oct, Wed & Sun
The workshops adjoin Parnham House, a fine Tudor manor house. Work in progress can be seen in the workshops and recently completed pieces are shown in the Tudor Great Hall. Monthly exhibition by eminent sculptor, artist, craftsman or designer. Collection of antique tools and wood craftsmanship. The School for Craftsmen in Wood is not open.

Berwick St. John

Guy R. H. Shaw
4 The Terrace, Berwick St John, nr Shaftesbury, Wiltshire. Tel Donhead 749
Small sculptures and carvings made from rare woods, ivory and stones. Work usually to commission.

Bickleigh

Bickleigh Mill Craft Centre and Farms
Bickleigh, nr Tiverton, Devon. Tel Bickleigh 419
Craft centre with workshops, craft shop and farm museum. Crafts include: pottery, glass engraving, jewellery, clay modelling, corn-dolly making, ceramic decoration, spinning and weaving, leatherwork and lace-making. The farm museum has displays on lace-making, thatching and cider-making.

Bossiney

Fenterleigh Woodcraft
Bossiney, nr Tintagel, Cornwall. Tel Camelford 770293
David Severn's workshop adjoins the showroom and work can be seen in progress. Besides his own furniture, rocking horses and small wooden pieces, also the work of other West Country craftsmen.

Bovey Tracey

Bovey Handloom Weavers
Bovey Tracey, nr Newton Abbot, Devon. Tel Bovey Tracey 833424
Manufacturers of handwoven pure wool tweeds, ties, scarves, and travelling rugs.

Lowerdown Pottery
Bovey Tracey, Devon. Tel Bovey Tracey 833408
This is the pottery of David Leach (whose father, Bernard, was one of the most influential figures in the studio pottery movement). The showroom is open for sale of thrown stoneware and porcelain. Workshop can be visited by appointment.

Bristol

Blaise Castle House Museum
Henbury, Bristol, Avon. Tel Bristol 506709. Easter-Sep, Sat-Wed 2-5; Oct-Easter, Mon-Sat 2-5
Collection illustrating English domestic life in 18th-c. house.

Bristol Craft Centre
6 Leonard Lane, Bristol, Avon. Tel Bristol 297890
Gallery has monthly exhibitions selling a variety of crafts. Resident craftsmen working in stained glass, hardwood furniture, leatherwork, appliqué, lace, embroidery and patchwork, porcelain, jewellery, exotic wood inlay and pottery.

Buckland St Mary

David Drew Basketmaker
Higher Hare Farm, Hare Lane, Buckland St Mary, nr Chard, Somerset. Tel Buckland St Mary 597
Using only Somerset willows, some of which he grows himself, David Drew makes traditional baskets.

Budleigh Salterton

Otterton Mill
nr Budleigh Salterton, Devon. Tel Colaton Raleigh 68521/68031
Work of the Mill's five craftsmen includes furniture for musicians, wood-turning, glass-blowing, pottery and spinning and weaving using wool from the Mill's flock of Shetland sheep. Craft shop and gallery with special exhibitions. Permanent exhibition of Honiton lace, with demonstrations of lace-making in summer.

Burrowbridge

W. Gadsby & Son
Burrowbridge, nr Bridgewater, Somerset. Tel Burrowbridge 259
Basket manufacturers making a large range of basketware and willow furniture from their own willows grown on the Somerset Levels.

Chudleigh

The Big Jug Craft Studio
31 Fore Street, Chudleigh, Devon. Tel Chudleigh 852191
Handthrown stoneware pottery and handloom weaving.

Clevedon

Clevedon Craft Centre
Newhouse Farm, Moor
Lane East, Clevedon, Avon.
Tel Clevedon 872567
14 studios include
workshops for the following
crafts: silver and jewellery,
tile tables, wax flowers,
wood turning and furniture
making, leatherwork, woodcarving, sculpted glass,
weaving and spinning, glass
engraving, calligraphy,
printing, cabinet making.
Also a small Countryside
Museum.

Crewkerne

Abbey Street Pottery
14 Abbey Street,
Crewkerne, Somerset. Tel
Crewkerne 74438.
Pottery shop selling the
work of Rory McLeod.
Using clays from Devon,
Dorset and Cornwall, he
makes stoneware cooking
pots, plates, mugs, bowls,
teapots, etc.

Dartington

The Cider Press Centre
Shinners Bridge,
Dartington, Totnes, Devon.
Tel Totnes 864171
Within the Dartington Hall
complex, this gallery sells
British crafts including a
full range of Dartington
pottery from the training
workshop next door.

Dorchester

*Ansty Pottery Studio
Workshop*
Ansty, nr Dorchester,
Dorset. Tel Milton Abbas
880 891
Ian Gregory's pottery,
where he makes salt-glazed
and domestic stoneware,
much in traditional West
Country forms.

Dulverton

Dulverton Weavers
The Studio, Dulverton,
Somerset
Specially designed clothes
woven and made up in a
range of wools and fibres,
including wool from Jacob
sheep and tussah silk.

Exeter

Palace Gate Gallery
1 Deanery Place, Palace
Gate, Exeter, Devon. Tel
Exeter 35978
Gallery specializing in
studio ceramics and hand-
blown glass.

Glastonbury

Somerset Rural Life Museum
Abbey Farm, Chilkwell
Street, Glastonbury,
Somerset. Tel Glastonbury
32903. Open daily
New museum in 14th-c.
abbey barn with courtyard
and outbuildings.
Exhibitions of rural life and
crafts. Demonstrations
during the summer.

Honiton

Allhallows Museum
High Street, Honiton,
Devon. Tel Honiton 307.
Easter, mid May-early Oct,
Mon-Sat 10-5
Display of local lace, with
lacemaking
demonstrations.

Ivybridge

Erme Wood Forge
Woodlands, Ivybridge,
Devon. Tel Ivybridge 2343
Forge making wrought
ironwork. Also porcelain
and furniture restoration.

Kingston St. Mary

Church Farm Weavers
Kingston St Mary, nr
Taunton, Somerset. Tel
Kingston St Mary 267
Handloom weaving by John
Lennon and Talbot Potter
who use some of their own
handspun wool, which they
also dye with plant dyes
such as heather, privet,
madder and walnut.

Lacock

Fournier Pottery
Tanyard, Lacock,
Wiltshire. Tel Lacock 266
Robert and Sheila Fournier
make tableware and
individual pieces in
stoneware and porcelain,
mostly thrown and some
handbuilt. Small showroom
usually open and pottery
when in use.

Maiden Newton

Warwick Parker
The Dairy House, Maiden
Newton, Dorchester,
Dorset. Tel Maiden Newton
414
A wide range of stoneware,
mostly wheel-thrown.

Marlborough

Katharine House Gallery
The Parade, Marlborough,
Wiltshire. Tel Marlborough
54397
Gallery specializing in
studio glass and ceramics.
Attached to the gallery is
the Litanus Press (visits by
prior arrangement).

Mere

Mitchell and Malik Ltd
The Workshop, Hazzards
Hill, Mere, nr Stourhead,
Wiltshire. Tel East Knoyle
504
Workshop produces
traditional hand-marbled
papers (open only by
arrangement).

Minehead

*McCoy Saddlery and
Leathercraft*
High Street, Porlock, nr
Minehead, Somerset. Tel
Minehead 862518
Manufacturers selling all
kinds of saddlery and
bridles as well as small
leather goods and handbags.
Workshop not open to the
public.

Modbury

Woodturners Craft Centre
New Road, Modbury,
Devon. Tel Modbury
830405
Open workshop showing
wood turning, carving and
furniture making.
Showroom sells woodwork
and other local crafts.

Okehampton

*Andrew Holden, South
Tawton Pottery*
South Tawton, nr
Okehampton, Devon. Tel
Sticklepath 609
Showroom with wide range
of domestic stoneware fired
in either a large oil-fired kiln
or a smaller wood-fired one.

Par
*Mid Cornwall Craft Centre
and Galleries*
Biscovey, nr Par, Cornwall.
Tel Par 2131
Changing exhibitions and
sale of work by artists and
craftsmen from the South
West; also weekly and daily
courses including pottery,
china painting, calligraphy
and painting.

Penzance
The Barbican
Battery Road, Penzance,
Cornwall. Tel Penzance
5610
Pottery making press-
moulded stoneware and
some decorative pieces.
Gallery sells other ceramic
works as well as paintings.
Also woodworker and area
with craft stalls.

Plymouth
Barbican Craft Workshops
1 White Lane, Barbican,
Plymouth, Devon. Tel
Plymouth 662338
Three resident craftsmen: a
potter, furniture maker and
weaver. Leatherwork,
wood turning and glass also
available in the showroom.

Polzeath
*Steve Walton and Jane
Thornton*
Chy-an-Mor, Polzeath, nr
Wadebridge, Cornwall. Tel
Trebetherick 2567
Leatherworkers producing
hand-stitched work of
modern and traditional
designs.

St Breward
Wenford Bridge Pottery
St Breward, nr Bodmin,
Cornwall. Tel Bodmin
850471
The pottery of Michael
Cardew who has worked
here since 1939, now with
his eldest son, Seth. They
prepare their own clays and
glazes, which mostly come
from the locality, e.g.
granite from St Breward for
glazes and local china clay.
The workshop is not on
view, but pottery can be
bought.

St Eval
St Eval Leather Crafts
Downhill, St Eval, nr
Wadebridge, Cornwall. Tel
St Mawgan 357
Leatherwork bags, purses,
bellows and other small
items, with plain and hand-
tooled finishes. Also
reproductions of medieval
leather vessels.

St Ives
*Cornwall Craft Association
Gallery*
Penwith Gallery, Back Road
West, St Ives, Cornwall
Quality craftwork made by
members of the Association.

*Kathryn Gregory and Robert
Floyd, Copper Enamellers*
Sloop Craft Market, St Ives,
Cornwall. Tel St Ives 6051
Pictures, brooches and pill-
boxes individually made and
enamelled with detailed
subjects of landscapes,
flowers and wild life.

Bryan Illsley
Higher Vorvas, Lelant, St
Ives, Cornwall. Tel St Ives
797145
Jeweller producing beaten
silver and gold, and hand-
ground and polished stones.

New Craftsman
24 Fore Street, St Ives,
Cornwall. Tel Penzance
795652
Craft shop and gallery
which sells the work of
important British potters.
Also weaving, jewellery,
paintings and prints.

Salcombe
Windjammer Gallery
Russell Court, Salcombe,
Devon. Tel Salcombe 2979
Gallery selling quality crafts
made in the West Country.
Behind the gallery is a slate
carver's studio.

Salisbury
Bill Toop Gallery
21 New Street, Salisbury,
Wiltshire. Tel Salisbury
20916
Watercolours, prints,
enamels and woodcuts. Also
stoneware, ceramics,
jewellery and wrought iron.

*Winstanley, Salisbury
Bookbinders*
213 Devizes Road,
Salisbury, Wiltshire. Tel
Salisbury 4998
Specialists in restoration
and conservation of
bindings and books (some
tools used date back to mid
19th c.). Rebound classics,
etc. for sale. If convenient,
the workshop may be
visited.

Somerton
Jacquie Baker
Weaver's Dream, Mill
Road, Barton St David,
Somerton, Somerset. Tel
Baltonsborough 50584
Using wool from her own
Dorset Horn sheep, Jacquie
Baker spins and weaves it
into tapestries. Also sells
handpainted lace bobbins.
Courses in spinning and
weaving.

Stogumber
Stogumber Woodwork
Wayshill, Stogumber, nr
Taunton, Somerset. Tel
Stogumber 205
Ralph Farrer makes
furniture to commission in
quality hardwood, also
stools, coffee tables, games
boards and other small
pieces which can be bought
from his showroom.

Stoke Gabriel
*Michael & Elizabeth
Skipwith*
The Pottery, Old Stoke
Farm, Stoke Gabriel, nr
Totnes, Devon. Tel Stoke
Gabriel 303
Produce pottery influenced
by 19th-c. red earthenware
Devon jugs, also stoneware
and porcelain. The Lotus
Gallery shows work of
Devon Guild of Craftsmen.

Tiverton
The English Lace School
42 St. Peter's Street,
Tiverton, Devon. Tel
Tiverton 53918
School teaching traditional
English lacemaking. Open
days on Bank Holiday
Mondays and special
exhibition in August.

Torrington
Dartington Glass and Glass Shop
Torrington, Devon. Tel
Torrington 3797
Handblown glass which
visitors can see being made
during guided tours of the
factory. Telephone to check
times of tours.

Trelowarren
*Cornwall Craft Association at
Trelowarren*
nr Helston, Cornwall
Display of member's work,
also exhibitions.

Truro
*Truro Pottery and Old Kiln
Museum*
Chapel Hill, Truro,
Cornwall. Tel Truro 2928
Handthrown pottery made
on a site that has been used
for the same purpose since
the late 17th c. Remains of
one of the original kilns can
be seen together with wares
from the earlier pottery.

Washaway
Pencarrow Gallery
Pencarrow House,
Washaway, nr Bodmin,
Cornwall
Sale of work by Cornwall
Craft Association members
in Georgian mansion open
to the public.

Williton
*David Winkley, Yellow
Pottery*
Lower Vellow, Williton, nr
Taunton, Somerset. Tel
Stogumber 458
Wide range of handthrown
ovenproof stoneware
kitchenware, decorated with
brushwork or wax-resist
decoration. Also individual
pieces in stoneware and
porcelain.

Wimborne
Wimborne Pottery
6 West Borough,
Wimborne, Dorset. Tel
Wimborne 887613
Workshop producing
thrown decorated
earthenware, including
commemorative plates.
Shop sells local crafts.

East Midlands

*Bedfordshire, Derbyshire, Hertfordshire,
Leicestershire, Lincolnshire, Nottinghamshire and
Northamptonshire*

This area covers a wide range of landscape
and townscape, through the great landed
estates ('The Dukeries') down to the flat
arable land of Lincolnshire and the
gentle Hertfordshire countryside. There
are a number of crafts traditional to the
area. One of these is pillow lacemaking, which
was concentrated in the area around Bedford,
Olney and Newport Pagnell. Nottingham has
long been a centre for hand-frame knitting and
machined lace. (The hand frame is a very
simple machine, which produces a knitted
stocking stitch. It was invented by the Rev.
William Lee of Calverton, Nottinghamshire in
1589. Like the handloom it was formerly part
of the furniture in many cottage homes,
particularly in this area.)

Northampton has been a tanning and
leatherworking (particularly boot and
shoemaking) centre since medieval times.
Bedfordshire has long been famous for its straw
products, in particular its plaited straw hats.

Alvingham
Alvingham Pottery
nr Louth, Lincolnshire. Tel
South Cockerington 230
Handthrown and decorated
earthenware. Decorative
techniques include wax-
resist and slip-trailing.

Baslow
The Derbyshire Craft Centre
Calver Bridge, nr Baslow,
Derbyshire. Tel Hope
Valley 31231
Shop selling a range of local
and national craftwork.

Barnet
Old Bull Gallery
68 High Street, Barnet,
Hertfordshire. Tel (01) 449
0048
There are two galleries in
the main building, one

showing exhibitions, the
other the work of local and
resident craftsmen. Craft
market on Saturdays. In
Old Bull Yard there are
workshops including a glass-
blower, guitar maker, potter
and silversmiths.

Bedford
Thomas Hudson
117 High Street, Odell, nr
Bedford. Tel Bedford
721133/720587
Woodworker specializing in
handmade furniture, church
woodwork, wall panelling
and incised lettering. Also
antique restoration.

Boston
Old Forge Woodturners
Sleaford Road, Swineshead
Bridge, nr Boston,
Lincolnshire. Tel Boston
820502
Old-established family
turnery making furniture,
children's furniture, table
and standard lamps.

Brackley
Duncan James, Jeweller
33 High Street, Brackley,
Northamptonshire. Tel
Brackley 703060
Duncan James produces a
wide range of jewellery in
gold, silver and precious
stones. Workshop can be
visited by appointment.

Brafield on the Green
Mildmay Pottery
12 Bridle Path, Brafield on
the Green,
Northamptonshire. Tel
Northampton 891488
Paul Ager's pottery, which
produces domestic
stoneware in two main
glazes.

Brigg
Elsham Forge
Elsham Hall Park, Brigg,
South Humberside.
Blacksmith producing
traditional wrought
ironwork.

Byfield
BW Pottery
32/4 Banbury Lane,
Byfield, nr Daventry,
Northamptonshire. Tel
Byfield 60630
Nigel Buchanan-
Wollaston's pottery, making
domestic stoneware which is
sold from the shop on the
premises.

Carburton
Wren Craftsmen
The Old School, Carburton,
Nottinghamshire. Tel
Worksop 483517
Makers of furniture in
English walnut and oak,
mostly from nearby
Sherwood Forest. Range of
typically English designs,
domestic pieces and church
furnishings.

Dove Holes
Alfred Bentley
New Forge, Beech Lane,
Dove Holes, nr Buxton,
Derbyshire. Tel Chapel-en-
le-Frith 812170
Smith using the traditional
methods, producing
traditional designs.

Elkesley
Chris Aston Pottery
4 High Street, Elkesley, nr
Retford, Nottinghamshire.
Tel Gamston 391
Thrown stoneware pottery
in a range of domestic and
individual pieces. Chris
Aston prepares own blend
of ball clay.

Ellastone
Yew Tree Gallery
The Square, Ellastone, nr
Ashbourne, Derbyshire.
Tel Ellastone 341
Shows and sells work by
artist-craftsmen from all
over the country. Special
exhibitions monthly,
usually one-man, of
jewellery, pottery, glass,
weaving, embroidery and so
on. Also paintings.
Occasional demonstrations.

Elvaston
Elvaston Castle Museum
Borrowash Road, Elvaston,
Derbyshire. Tel Derby
73799. Easter-Oct 31, Wed-
Sat 1-5, Sun & Bank Hols
10-6
Recreates life on an
agricultural estate at the
beginning of 20th c.
Includes displays and
demonstrations in the estate
craft workshops:
blacksmith, farrier, joiner,
saddler and cobbler.

Grane Mill
Nigel Griffiths
The Old Cheese Factory,
Grange Mill, nr Matlock,
Derbyshire. Tel Winster
720
Furniture maker producing
handmade oak furniture,
mainly dressers, refectory
tables, chairs and
sideboards. Workshop and
showroom.

Grimsby
*David Morris and Avril
Morris*
Archways, Caistor Road,
Laceby, Grimsby, South
Humberside. Tel Grimsby
72341
David Morris produces a
range of domestic pottery,
stoneware glazed white with
blue brushed decoration.
Avril Morris makes pierrot
wall plaques and other
ceramic modelling. Small
showroom. Workshop and
pottery not normally open.

Grindleford
*Andrew Lawton, Furniture
Maker*
The Workshop, Goatscliff,
Grindleford, Derbyshire.
Tel Chesterfield 202 822
(eves)
Handmade furniture and
woodwork in solid
hardwoods using traditional
techniques allied to
progressive design.
Workshop has been used for
same purpose for over 60
years.

Heckington
*The Pearoom Craft Heritage
Centre*
Station Yard, Station Road,
Heckington, Sleaford,
Lincolnshire. Tel Sleaford
60765
19th-c. pea-sorting
warehouse converted by the
Heckington Village Trust
into craft workshops,
exhibition space and sales
gallery. Craftsmen include a
stained glass artist,
woodworker, leatherworker
and caneworker. The
Lincolnshire Guild of
Spinners, Weavers and
Dyers is also based here and
classes in these and other
crafts are held.

Kirton in Lindsey
Kirton Pottery
36 High Street, Kirton in
Lindsey, Lincolnshire. Tel
Kirton in Lindsey 648867
Produces domestic pottery
in stoneware and traditional
English slipware, some
sculptural pieces.

Lambley
The Lambley Pottery Shop
102 Main Street, Lambley.
Tel Burton Joyce 2777
Wide range of handmade
ceramics from earthenware
to stoneware to porcelain.

Lincoln
Regional Craft Centre
Jews Court, Steep Hill,
Lincoln. Tel Lincoln 33247
Centre for Lincolnshire and
Humberside Arts. Sales area
for local crafts, and two
exhibition spaces.
Occasional demonstrations,
but telephone for details.

Luton
*Luton Museum and Art
Gallery*
Wardown Park, Luton,
Bedfordshire. Tel Luton
36941/2. Mon-Sat 10-6, Sun
2-6 (Oct-Mar closes at 5);
closed Dec 25 & 26, Jan 1,
also Suns in Dec & Jan.
Museum showing the
history and archaeology of
the area. Special displays on
the local pillow lace makers.

Matlock
Prisms Studio
41 St Joseph's Street,
Matlock, Derbyshire. Tel
Matlock 2782
David Prytherch and Judith
Harris are glass engravers,
and the studio is open to the
public.

Northampton
Four Seasons Gallery
39 St Giles Street,
Northampton. Tel
Northampton 32287
Craft gallery showing a wide
selection of pottery, glass,
wood, jewellery, etc. Gallery
of contemporary prints.

Museum of Leathercraft
The Old Bluecoat School,
Bridge Street,
Northampton. Tel
Northampton 34881. Mon-
Sat 10-1, 2-5.30
Museum of the history of
leather craftsmanship up to
the present, with fine
examples of harness,
saddlery, luggage, costume,
caskets and bindings.

*Central Museum and Art
Gallery*
Guildhall Rd, Northampton.
Tel Northampton 34881.
Mon-Sat 10-6
Special collection of
footwear through the ages.
Cobbler's workshop.

Nottingham
Focus Gallery
108 Derby Road,
Nottingham. Tel
Nottingham 417913
Craft shop and gallery with
ceramics, jewellery, wood
carvings, glass, paintings,
sculpture and prints.

Nottingham Lace Centre
Severns Building, Castle
Road, Nottingham. Tel
Nottingham 413539
Exhibition and sale of local
lace, both machine-made
and knitted on handframes.

Ollerton
Rufford Craft Centre
Rufford Country Park,
Ollerton, Nottinghamshire.
Tel Mansfield 822944
Gallery with exhibitions of
craftwork and paintings.
Shop sells work by national
and local craftsmen.

Pavenham
P. M. Morgan
Mill Lane, Pavenham,
Bedfordshire. Tel Oakley
2393
Using rushes cut from the
nearby river Ouse, Mrs
Morgan does rushwork of
all kinds, including baskets
and chairseating.

Peterborough
S. W. Halford & Son
8 South Street, Crowland,
Lincolnshire. Tel
Peterborough 210605
Hand-stitched harnesses,
saddles and bridles.

Ravenshead
Ravenshead Pottery
23 Milton Drive,
Ravenshead,
Nottinghamshire. Tel
Blidworth 3178
Joan and Brian Marris
produce decorative and
domestic stoneware pottery.

Ruddington
Framework Knitters' Museum
Chapel Street, Ruddington,
Nottinghamshire. Tel
Nottingham 212116. Wed
7-9, or by appointment
Early 19th-c. framework
knitter and hosier's cottage
with working machinery.

Rushden
*Woodware and Maple
Products*
Rushden Road,
Wymington, Rushden,
Northamptonshire. Tel
Rushden 316555
Handmade furniture in oak,
mahogany or pine.

St Albans
City Museum
Hatfield Road, St Albans,
Hertfordshire. Tel St
Albans 56679. Mon-Sat 10-5
Salaman collection of tools,
some of which are arranged
in workshops, (blacksmith's,
wheelwright's etc.).

Stotfold
Ironcrafts
Baldock Road, Stotfold,
Bedfordshire. Tel Baldock
730671
Wrought ironworkers,
making balustrading, gates,
grates, grilles. If convenient,
the forge can be seen.

Scunthorpe
Normanby Hall
Scunthorpe, Humberside.
Tel Scunthorpe 720215.
Apr-Oct, Mon-Sat 10-
12.30, 2-5.30 (closed Tue
and sometimes Sat, check in
advance), Sun 2-5; Nov-
Mar, Mon-Fri 10-12.30, 2-
5, Sun 2-5
Pottery and working
blacksmith set in grounds of
Regency house.

Skegness
Millstone Craft Centre
Mill House, West End,
Hogsthorpe, Lincolnshire.
Tel Skegness 72977
Stuart Macdonald's pottery
producing oxidised
stoneware, including a large
range of individually
decorated vases.

Sudbury
Museum of Childhood
Sudbury Hall, Sudbury,
Derbyshire. Tel Sudbury
305. Apr-Oct, Wed-Sun &
Bank Hol Mons 1-5.30 (or
dusk, if earlier)
Charles II house with fine
woodcarving and
plasterwork, containing
museum of toys, games etc.
Also collection of 20th-c.
studio pottery.

Ware
Albert Springate
The Forge, Dane End,
Ware, Hertfordshire. Tel
Dane End 227
Traditional blacksmith
working in premises that
have been used as a forge
since the early 18th c. Also
makes iron sculpture.

Whipsnade
Whipsnade Gallery
The Old Rectory,
Whipsnade, Bedfordshire.
Tel Whipsnade 872743
Shop in 17th-c. house
showing collection of
pottery, ceramics, wood,
leather, glass, weaving,
jewellery and local lace.
Occasional demonstrations.

Wirksworth
Frank Pratt
Old Grammar School,
Church Walk, Wirksworth,
Derbyshire. Tel
Wirksworth 2828
T. C. Jones, craftsman in
wood, makes hand-carved
traditional English
furniture.

Youlgrave
Asquith Silver
Turret House, Youlgrave,
nr Bakewell, Derbyshire.
Tel Youlgrave 204
Silver workshop making
both holloware (bowls,
goblets, etc.) and jewellery.
Some work combines silver
with local minerals such as
Blue John, and various local
marbles. At the same
address is the *Middleton
Forge* making hand-forged
ironwork: gates, screens,
garden furniture, etc.

West Midlands

*Cheshire, Gloucestershire, Herefordshire,
Shropshire, Staffordshire, Warwickshire and
Hereford & Worcester*

This area contains within it some of the richest
farmland of England, in particular the fruit
orchards of Hereford and Worcester. But it is
also where the Industrial Revolution began,
stimulated by the area's natural resources.
Thus, in the middle of the 17th century the
area around Stoke-on-Trent became the centre
of the pottery industry, and work continued to
be handmade until Josiah Wedgwood
introduced mass-manufacturing towards the
end of the 18th century. During the same
period, Birmingham became the centre for
metalworking, first iron and steel, then copper,
brass and ormolu.

The glass made in the Stourbridge area during
the 19th century is some of the most
remarkable and experimental made in Britain.
Though these centres are now dominated by
mass-production and industrial life, each area
has strong links with its early craft origins. The
local museums have excellent collections of this
early work and some have been pioneers in
bringing craftsmen into museums to practise
their skills and save disappearing techniques.

Acton Scott
*Acton Scott Working Farm
Museum*
Wenlock Lodge, Acton
Scott, nr Church Stretton,
Shropshire. Tel
Marshbrook 306/7. Apr-
Oct, daily
Museum of agriculture at
the turn of the century.
Programme of craft
demonstrations. Shop.

Bewdley
Bewdley Museum
The Shambles, Load Street,
Bewdley, Hereford &
Worcester. Tel Bewdley
403573. Mar-Nov, Mon-Sat
10-5.30, other
times by appointment
Late-18th-c. market

converted into folk and local
history museum which
depicts crafts and industries
of Bewdley and Wyre
Forest. Studios within the
museum sometimes have
demonstrations by
craftsmen.

Bibury
Arlington Mill Museum
Bibury, Gloucestershire.
Tel Bibury 368. Mar-Oct,
daily 10.30-7; Nov-Feb,
weekends only
Museum of rural crafts and
industries within 17th-c.
corn mill. Mill machinery
still extant. Special display
of Arts and Crafts
Movement material.

Birmingham
Birmingham Museum and Art Gallery
Chamberlain Square, Birmingham B3 3DH. Tel Birmingham 235 2834. Mon-Sat 10-5.30, Sun 2-5.30; closed Good Fri, Dec 25 & 26, Jan 1
Of particular interest: the Pinto Collection of Wooden Bygones, an extremely rich and varied collection of turned and carved wood.

Spock Woodcarvings
810 Bristol Road, Selly Oak, Birmingham. Tel Birmingham 472 4969
Craftsman in wood, working on the premises. Shop sells local crafts: stained glass, ceramics, wooden toys, enamels. Working museum featuring a blacksmith's forge planned for Spring 1983.

Bourton-on-the-Water
Chestnut Gallery
High Street, Bourton-on-the-Water, Gloucestershire. Tel Bourton-on-the-Water 20017
Shop specializing in studio pottery, also selling studio glass, ceramic sculpture, jewellery and turned wood. Occasional special exhibitions.

Bromsgrove
Avoncroft Museum of Buildings
Stoke Heath, Bromsgrove, Hereford & Worcester. Tel Bromsgrove 31363/31886. Mar-Nov, daily 10.30-5.30 (or dusk, if earlier)
Open air museum with a collection of vernacular buildings. Working forge, also fully equipped workshops where nails and chains were made by hand.

Cauldon Lowe
Staffordshire Peak Arts Centre
The Old School, Cauldon Lowe, nr Waterhouses, Staffordshire. Tel Waterhouses 431
Large selection of crafts. Special exhibitions, some with demonstrations.

Chester
Three Kings Studios
90-92 Lower Bridge Street, Chester, Shropshire. Tel Chester 317717
Recently restored Tudor building houses the studios of Tony Eaton, potter, and Margaret Eaton, embroiderer. They can be seen working from the shop which also sells the work of local craftsmen. Special exhibitions, sometimes accompanied by demonstrations.

Chipping Campden
Campden Weavers
High Street, Chipping Campden, Gloucestershire. Tel Evesham 840864
Shop selling handwoven and handknitted articles in this medieval wool town.

Cirencester
The Cirencester Workshops
Brewery Court, Cricklade Street, Cirencester, Gloucestershire. Tel Cirencester 61566
11 separate workshops, each open to the public for a minimum of eight hours a week, so visitors can always see something. Crafts include: pottery, jewellery, caning, basket making, furniture making, leatherworker, weaving, knitting, bookbinding, illustration.
   Also a gallery with a programme of changing exhibitions of work by artist-craftsmen and a shop selling toys, furniture, textiles, leather, glass, jewellery, marbled papers, etc.

Coventry
Centre Crafts
169 Spon Street, Coventry, West Midlands. Tel Coventry 27200
In one of Coventry's oldest surviving buildings a 14th-c. house, gallery with carefully chosen selection of quality work by artist-craftsmen: ceramics, studio glass, wood, leather, jewellery and textiles. Two special exhibitions a year.

Dudley
Broadfield House Glass Museum
Compton Drive, Kingswinford, Dudley, West Midlands. Tel Dudley 43011. Tue-Fri 2-6, Sat 10-1, 2-5. Sun 2-5
New museum specializing in the achievements of the local glassmakers, particularly of the 19th c. Glassmaking studio and glass engraver working within the museum, also museum shop selling the work of modern glass craftsmen.

Farndon
Cheshire Craft Centre
High Street, Farndon, nr Chester, Cheshire. Tel Farndon 270936
Selection of British crafts, also sale of craft materials. Three workshops in converted barn where work can be seen in progress. Demonstrations by arrangement.

Gloucester
Folk Museum
99-103 Westgate Street, Gloucester. Tel Gloucester 26467. Mon-Sat 10-5, Sun in Aug 2-5
Tudor buildings with exhibition of local crafts, trades and industries.

Hanbury
Jinney Ring Craft Centre
Hanbury Road, Hanbury, nr Bromsgrove, Hereford & Worcester. Tel Hanbury 272
Eight workshops in restored farm buildings, with crafts including: stained glass, jewellery, weaving, blown glass, woodcarving, toys, porcelain and porcelain dolls, wood turning. Permanent exhibition of old farm implements. Shop.

Henley-in-Arden
Torquil Pottery
81 High Street, Henley-in-Arden, Warwickshire. Tel Henley-in-Arden 2174
Reg Moon's pottery, producing handmade stoneware and porcelain.

Horsley
Rosemary Gill
Old White Hart, Downend,
Horsley, nr Stroud,
Gloucestershire. Tel
Nailsworth 3554
Quilting and patchwork,
using new interpretations of
traditional patchwork and
appliqué designs. Also
individually designed
clothes.

Ipstones
Rookes Pottery
High Street, Ipstones,
Stoke-on-Trent,
Staffordshire. Tel Ipstones
606
Using local clay, this
pottery makes handthrown
terracotta garden pots and
domestic stoneware.

Kenilworth
Sylvia Hardaker, Kenilworth Pottery
186 Warwick Road,
Kenilworth, Warwickshire.
Tel Kenilworth 512314
Range of stoneware pots
from domestic to individual
pieces. Telephone for
appointment.

Kineton
Alan Murphy, Furniture Maker
Minshull House, Southam
Street, Kineton,
Warwickshire. Tel Kineton
641293
Furniture maker whose
work lays emphasis on
functional pieces made in
fine wood – mostly English
hardwoods. Workshop can
be visited by appointment.

Ledbury
Collection
13 The Southend, Ledbury,
Herefordshire. Tel Ledbury
3581
Shop selling handmade
pottery, woodware, glass
and baskets (which are
locally made). Work tends
to be functional. Also cards,
stationery, brass boxes and
paperweights from their
own workshops. Special
exhibitions three times a
year.

Newent
Cowdy Glass Workshop
27 Culver Street, Newent,
Gloucestershire. Tel
Newent 821173
Group of glassmakers
producing an original range
of drinking glasses, vases,
paperweights, etc.
Workshop, showroom and
gallery combined.

Ombersley
Ombersley Galleries
Church Terrace,
Ombersley, Hereford &
Worcester. Tel Worcester
620655
Gallery with a wide range of
crafts for sale: batik,
jewellery, leather, wood,
engraved and cut glass,
spinning, weaving, wood
turning, small furniture,
pottery, rushwork,
embroidery and knitting.

Oswestry
The Hengoed Pottery
Hilbre, Hengoed,
Oswestry, Shropshire. Tel
Oswestry 59782
Peggy and Cyril Charlton's
pottery where they make a
range of stoneware birds
modelled from the wildlife
around them. Also vases,
plant pots, etc.

Ross-on-Wye
J. Arthur Wells
Gatsford, Ross-on-Wye,
Herefordshire. Tel Ross-on-
Wye 62595
Woodworker who makes
furniture and special pieces
to commission. Also treen
(turned wooden items).

Shrewsbury
St Julian's Craft Centre for Shropshire
St Julian's Church,
Shrewsbury, Shropshire.
Tel Shrewsbury 53516
Church in the centre of
town converted into 11
studios occupied by
working craftsmen,
including: woodworkers,
printer, spinner and weaver,
shoemaker and jeweller.
Craft market with additional
stalls every other Saturday.

Stafford
Stafford Museum and Art Gallery
The Green, Stafford. Tel
Stafford 57303. Tue-Sat
10-5
Local history museum and
art gallery with occasional
craft exhibitions. Shop.

Stinchcombe
The Cider Mill Gallery
Blanchworth, Stinchcombe,
Gloucestershire. Tel
Dursley 2352
Art gallery, and shop selling
pottery, patchwork, wood
turning, jewellery, etc. A
horse-drawn cider mill and
press have been restored
and produce traditional
farmhouse cider. (Jan, Feb
and Mar open only by
appointment.)

Stockport
Rock Craft Centre
Rock Buildings, Hooper
Street, Stockport, Cheshire.
Centre with six workshops,
including a furniture maker
and ceramist. Work can be
bought directly from the
craftsmen.

Stockton
Neville Neal
High Street, Stockton, nr
Rugby, Warwickshire. Tel
Southam 3702
Neville Neal and his son
Lawrence work to
traditional chair patterns:
ladder and spindle backs
with rush seats. They make
rocking, dining and
children's chairs and stools.
All their materials are local;
they use ash timber, and
rushes from local rivers.

Stoke-on-Trent
Gladstone Pottery Museum
Uttoxeter Road, Longton,
Stoke-on-Trent,
Staffordshire. Tel Stoke
319232. Mon-Sat 10.30-
5.30, (Oct-Mar closed
Mon), Sun & Bank hols 2-6
Although the museum
specializes in industrial
potteries, it does have
exhibits relating to earlier
periods. Demonstrations
and shop.

City Museum and Art Gallery
Broad Street, Hanley,
Stoke-on-Trent,
Staffordshire. Tel Stoke
29611 ext 2358. Mon-Sat
10.30-5 (Wed to 8)
New museum with one of
the largest collections of
English pottery and
porcelain, primarily from
the local potteries.

Stratford-upon-Avon
The Arden Pottery
31 Henley Street, Stratford-
upon-Avon, Warwickshire.
Tel Stratford-upon-Avon
4638
Barbara Cass produces
handthrown stoneware,
mainly individual pieces,
and specializes in wood ash
glazes.

Peter Dingley
16 Meer Street, Stratford-
upon-Avon, Warwickshire.
Tel Stratford-upon-Avon
5001
Ground floor sells mixture
of work by artist-craftsmen.
Upper floor has four one-
man exhibitions a year and a
special ceramics exhibition
each summer.

Soft Surround
Studio Two, Centre Craft
Yard, Henley Street,
Stratford-upon-Avon,
Warwickshire. Tel
Stratford-upon-Avon
295070
Craft shop and gallery
which specializes in work in
textiles by artist-craftsmen.
They also stock modern
jewellery, prints, pictures
and dolls.

Stroud
Dennis French Woodware
The Craft Shop, Rock
House, Brimscombe Hill,
nr Stroud, Gloucestershire.
Tel Brimscombe 883054
Using elm, yew, sycamore,
beech and ash, Dennis
French produces domestic
turned wood pieces such as
salad bowls, lamp bases,
platters, scoops, etc. Shop
also sells local pottery and
baskets. Workshop only
open by arrangement.

Traditional Derbyshire carved chair

Styal
Quarry Bank Mill
Styall, nr Wilmslow,
Cheshire. Apr-Sep, Tue-
Sun & Bank Hol Mon in
Jul, 11-5; Mar, Oct, Nov,
Tue-Sun 12-4.30; Dec, Jan,
Feb, Sat and Sun 12-4.30;
closed Dec 25
Industrial Revolution mill
and village. The Georgian
cotton mill is now a working
museum of the early cotton
industry. Also frequent
spinning and weaving
demonstrations on hand and
power looms.
Styal Workshop is attached
to the museum. Visitors can
book for an afternoon or
morning of practical work:
spinning, weaving, printing
and dyeing are all taught.
Also specialist courses and
regular classes.

Warmingham
*Warmingham Craft
Workshops*
The Mill, Warmingham, nr
Sandbach, Cheshire. Tel
Warmingham 304
Workshops of a silversmith,
cabinet and furniture
maker, potter, model maker
and framer, also a part-time
blacksmith. Gallery has a
big display of local crafts,
including items by resident
craftsmen.

Wightwick
Wightwick Pottery
Wightwick, nr
Wolverhampton,
Staffordshire
Thrown stoneware with
brown, green and oatmeal
glazes, and earthenware
with lip and sgraffito
decoration. Press-moulded
plates.

Winchcombe
Winchcombe Pottery
Winchcombe, nr
Cheltenham,
Gloucestershire. Tel
Winchcombe 602462
On the site of an old country
pottery dating back to the
early 1800s. Ray Finch and
five other potters at
Winchcombe now produce a
wide range of handthrown,
wood-fired, stoneware pots.
Shop also shows the work of
a furniture maker and wood
turner. The workshop is
usually open to visitors.

The North and Isle of Man

Cumbria, County Durham, Humberside, Lancashire, Merseyside, Northumberland, Yorkshire and Tyne & Wear

Much of the country in Northern England is hilly and rugged, and is traditionally sheep country: the Borders, the West Riding of Yorkshire and the Lake District. Wool dominates the crafts of the area – spinning, weaving and knitting. Not only did sheep thrive on the uplands, but the water of the Pennine streams was soft and perfect for washing the wool in preparation for these later stages. Although the cotton industry of Lancashire is clearly not a hand craft, Northern craftwork is famous for its textiles. An example of this is the exquisite quilting which was traditional to the area around Durham.

There is evidence of cutlery being made in Sheffield as early as the 14th century. The city is now famous for its manufactured metalwork, particularly steel and silver, but , there are still craftsmen who work these famous materials.

The Isle of Man is ideal country for sheep-rearing. This is reflected in the crafts of spinning and weaving which have long been established there. The island has many Celtic relics – in particular Celtic stone monuments – and this has inspired many Manx craftworkers of today.

Addingham
Helyg Pottery and Textile Workshop
2 Bolton Road, Addingham, nr Ilkley, West Yorkshire. Tel Addingham 830165
The pottery of Eric Stockl, who makes functional stoneware and large individual pieces with a wide range of glazes. Meira Stockl does tapestry weaving and some collage, also rugs and bags. Shop stocks a wide variety of work.

Bacup
Derek Clarkson
1 The Poplars, Bacup, Lancashire. Tel Bacup 874541
Potter who makes individual pieces in stoneware and porcelain, mostly bottles, bowls and lidded jars. Brush and wax-resist decoration, also classic glazes such as celadon, tenmoku and chun.

Barnard Castle
Kenneth G. Shepherd
7 Teesdale Road, Startforth, Barnard Castle, County Durham. Tel Teesdale 37754
Designer and maker of handmade jewellery who also repairs and restores small silver pieces. Workshop not open to the public.

Bedale
Robin Watson Signs
Robin's Return, Hunton, Bedale, North Yorkshire. Tel Bedale 50388/50514
Makers of carved wooden signs, also barometers and marine and kitchen clocks. Wood engraving, turning and carving can be seen.

Brampton
Frank Mercer Handloom Weaver
Eastern Cottage, Hallbankgate, Brampton, Cumbria. Tel Brampton 309
Makes handwoven lengths of woollen cloth suitable for men's and women's clothes. The wool is mainly from Cheviot or Scottish sheep.

Coxwold
Coxwold Pottery
Coxwold, nr York. Tel Coxwold 344
Peter Dick's pottery, which makes a wide range of useful earthenware and stoneware pots for kitchen, table and garden with slip-trailed and impressed decoration. Stewpots and mixing bowls are based on traditional Yorkshire forms.

Darlington
Darlington Arts Centre
Vane Terrace, Darlington, County Durham. Tel Darlington 483271
Incorporated into the Arts Centre there is a craft shop which sells work by resident craftsmen, including: ceramic sculptor, weaver, jeweller, embroiderer, furniture maker, leatherworker, wildlife artist. Occasional demonstrations and monthly craft fairs.

Dent
Dent Crafts Centre
Dent, nr Sedburgh,
Cumbria. Tel Dent 210
Hand-printer Brian Bradley
works on Columbian,
Albion and Arab presses
using Victorian type. Sells
clothes handknitted from
the wool of Jacob sheep.
Two potters, a silversmith
and a machine knitter also
have workshops on the
premises.

Doncaster
Puzzleplex
Stubbs Walden, Doncaster,
South Yorkshire. Tel
Doncaster 700997
Peter Stocken handmakes
three-dimensional wooden
puzzles in a variety of local
and rare foreign hardwoods.

Driffield
Oak Rabbit Crafts
Wetwang, Driffield, North
Humberside. Tel Driffield
86257
Woodworkers in English
oak make furniture and
grandfather clocks, as well
as smaller turned pieces,
bowls, breadboards, etc.

Everton
*Jane Hamlyn, Millfield
Pottery*
Everton, South Yorkshire.
Tel Wiseton 723
Pottery specializing in
salt-glazed stoneware and
porcelain.

Gateshead
*Shipley Museum & Art
Gallery*
Prince Consort Road South,
Gateshead, Tyne & Wear.
Tel Gateshead 771495.
Mon-Fri 10-6, Sun 2-5
A growing collection of
contemporary crafts:
traditional and modern,
regional and national.

Grasmere
White Bridge Forge
Grasmere, Cumbria. Tel
Grasmere 414
Alan Ellwood's forge where
he makes fire-dogs, grates,
ram's-head pokers, wall
lights and brackets.

Grewelthorpe
Grewelthorpe Handweavers
Grewelthorpe, nr Ripon,
North Yorkshire. Tel
Kirkby Malzeard 209
Workshop and craft shop.
Handwoven cloth, wall-
hangings, ties, etc.

Halifax
The Piece Hall
Halifax, West Yorkshire.
Mon-Sat 11-5, Sun 10-5
The Piece Hall originally
opened in 1779 for the sale
of cloth manufactured on
hand looms by local
weavers. Now a textile
museum.

West Yorkshire Folk Museum
Shibden Hall, Shibden
Park, Halifax, West
Yorkshire. Tel Halifax
52246. Apr-Sep, Mon-Sat
11-7, Sun 2-5; Oct-Nov,
Mar, Mon-Sat 11-5, Sun 2-
5; Feb, Sun only
Museum displays early
agricultural implements,
coaches and harnesses and
craft workshops.

Hawes
*W. R. Outhwaite & Son,
Ropemakers*
Town Foot, Hawes, North
Yorkshire. Tel Hawes 487
Manufacture of rope, cord
and twine by traditional
methods.

Upper Dales Folk Museum
Station Road, Hawes,
North Yorkshire. Tel
Hawes 494. Apr-Sep, Mon-
Sat 11-1, 2-5, Sun 1-5; Oct,
Tue, Sat & Sun
Museum illustrating life in
the area, notably sheep
farming and use of wool for
knitting.

Holmfirth
Booth House Gallery
3 Booth House Lane,
Holmfirth, near
Huddersfield, West
Yorkshire. Tel Holmfirth
5270
Jim Robinson produces
ceramic sculpture and
functional ceramic ware.
Other craftwork, e.g. rugs,
for sale. Pottery can be
visited by appointment.

Hutton-le-Hole
Ryedale Folk Museum
Hutton-le-Hole, North
Yorkshire.Tel
Kirbymoorside 5367.
Apr-Oct, daily 11-6
Museum of rural life with
extensive collection of 19th-
c. craft tools. In the grounds
there is a collection of
buildings, including a
blacksmith's shop and an
early glass kiln.

Ireshopeburn
Michael and Mary Crompton
Forge Cottage,
Ireshopeburn, nr Bishop
Auckland, County Durham.
Tel Weardale 537346
Workshop for hand-
spinning and weaving. Also
day courses.

Kendal
*Abbot Hall Art Gallery &
Museum of Lakeland Life
and Industry*
Kendal, Cumbria Tel
Kendal 22464. Mon-Fri
10.30-5.30, Sat & Sun 2-5.
Display of decorative arts
and special local crafts, *The
Shop* in the museum sells
work by Lake District
craftsmen: rugs, patchwork,
pottery, glass, jewellery,
toys.

Kendal
Susan Foster, Weaver
9 Windemere Road,
Kendal, Cumbria. Tel
Kendal 26494
Specializes in floor rugs
and cushions, also wall-
hangings, belts, bags, etc.
Wool from the local
Herdwick and Swaledale
sheep is sometimes used.
Weaving and spinning
supplies are also sold from
the showroom.

Kilburn
*Robert Thompson's
Craftsmen*
Kilburn, York. Tel
Coxwold 218
Grandsons of Robert
Thompson run a large
workshop making
traditional domestic and
ecclesiastical oak furniture,
each piece carved with their
trademark of a mouse.

Leeds
Anno Domini
249 Otley Road, Leeds,
West Yorkshire. Tel Leeds
755059
Ann O'Donnell's handmade
jewellery uses gold, silver,
precious and semi-precious
stones, also uncut crystals
and fossils from Yorkshire.
Work of other jewellers also
shown.

Littlebeck
Littlebeck Craftsmen
Woodcarvers Shop,
Littlebeck, nr Whitby,
North Yorkshire. Tel
Sleights 224
Using local oak, church and
domestic furniture is made
and carved by traditional
methods.

Liverpool
Bluecoat Display Centre
School Lane, Liverpool,
Merseyside. Tel Liverpool
709 4014
Non-profitmaking craft
centre showing and selling
the work of British artist-
craftsmen.

Editions Gallery
12 Commutation Row,
Liverpool 1, Merseyside.
Tel Liverpool 207 0221
Gallery for fine art and
prints. Also shop, stocking
jewellery, ceramics and
glass.

Manchester
Lantern Gallery Crafts Centre
3 Worsley Road, Worsley,
Manchester. Tel
Manchester 794 8956
Gallery with exhibitions of
local craftwork; also three
workshops (one a jeweller)
where work can be seen in
progress and purchased.

Marsett
Douglas Owen, Woodturner
Green View, Marsett,
Bainbridge, North
Yorkshire. Tel Wensleydale
50485
Works in a wide range of
local and imported woods,
producing eggs, bowls,
ornamental fruit, scoops,
stools, etc.

Newcastle upon Tyne
Blackfriars Craft Centre
Stowell Street, Newcastle
upon Tyne, Tyne & Wear.
Tel Newcastle 614307
Several craftsmen work on
the premises. Shop sells
pottery, leather, textiles,
jewellery, glass, prints,
toys, batik, enamel, corn
dollies, patchwork and
wood.

Ossett
J. Burdekin Ltd
Basket Works, Ossett, West
Yorkshire. Tel Wakefield
273103
Basket manufacturers who
produce many items for
industry, including the local
textile industry, but also
make log, shopping and
linen baskets. Large
showroom displays their
own products, as well as
imported basketware and
cane furniture. Works only
open by arrangement.

Otley
Curlew Pottery
11 Crossgate, Otley, West
Yorkshire. Tel Otley
464188
K. M. Hunter's studio
pottery, making
handthrown domestic ware,
also individual pieces.

Padiham
Gawthorpe Hall
Padiham, Lancashire. Tel
Nelson 78511. Mid-Mar-
Oct, Wed, Sat, Sun & Bank
Hol Mon 2-6; also Tue in
Jul, Aug
National Trust house with
special collection of
needlework and lace. *Coach
House Craft Gallery* has a
wide selection of work by
professional craftsmen.
Monthly exhibitions.

Pilling
Pilling Pottery
School Lane, Pilling, nr
Garstang, Lancashire. Tel
Pilling 307
Shows a large range of
handthrown pottery: over
60 different forms and
shapes are regularly
produced and stocked.

Powburn
Breamish Vallery Pottery
Branton, Powburn, nr
Alnwick, Northumberland.
Tel Powburn 263
Alastair Hardie's pottery,
where he produces a full
range of handmade kitchen
and domestic stoneware
using a wood-fired kiln.

Scarborough
Crescent Arts Workshop
The Crescent, Scarborough,
North Yorkshire.
Workshops in the basement
of the Art Gallery for:
jeweller, potter, printer,
furniture designer, sculptor.
The workshops are also
used by other craftsmen on
a part-time basis.

Shap
Shap Pottery
1 Central Buildings, Shap,
Cumbria. Tel Shap 412
Workshop open to show
potters Bob and Lynne
Entwistle making
traditional domestic
pottery. Slip-trailed and
decorated earthenware can
be bought.

Sheffield
Yorkshire Art Space Society
Sydney Works, 111 Matilda
Street, Sheffield 1, South
Yorkshire. Tel Sheffield
71769
Sydney Works houses 46
artists and craftsmen,
including: silversmiths,
jewellers, bronze caster,
clock maker, furniture
designer, potter, and
designer of pen and pocket
knives. Gallery sells their
work.

Silverdale
Wolf House Gallery
Nr Jenny Browns Point,
Gibraltar, Silverdale, nr
Lancaster, Lancashire. Tel
Silverdale 701405
Showing mainly work by
Northern craftsmen and
artists: handblown glass,
weaving, leather, wooden
toys, pottery etc. Frank
Irving has his pottery on the
premises, and makes
decorated earthenware.

Simonstone
Trapp Forge
Simonstone, nr Burnley,
Lancashire. Tel Padiham
71025
Ron Carter's forge makes all
kinds of wrought ironwork:
fire-dogs, fire-irons, gates,
staircases, weather vanes,
signs, brackets, etc. The
showroom attached to the
forge also sells copper and
brassware.

Staveley
Peter Hall Woodcraft
Danes Road, Staveley, nr
Kendal, Cumbria. Tel
Kendal 821633
Domestic furniture made in
local oak, also imported
mahogany. Work in modern
and traditional styles (some
with carving in the manner
of 17th-c. strapwork). Large
pieces made to order but a
selection of small items can
be bought directly from the
workshop.

Sunderland
Ceolfrith Gallery
Sunderland Arts Centre, 27
Stockton Road,
Sunderland, Tyne &
Wear. Tel Sunderland
41214
There are four galleries
within the Art Centre. One
specializes in craft
exhibitions which are wide-
ranging and cover many
aspects of design and
contemporary craft work.

Thirsk
Albert Jeffray
Sessay, Thirsk, North
Yorkshire. Tel Thirsk
401323
Furniture maker,
ecclesiastical and domestic,
English oak a speciality.
Woodcarving also done.

Tweedmouth
*Meadow Cottage Craft
Workshops*
Knowehead, Tweedmouth,
nr Berwick upon Tweed,
Northumberland. Tel
Berwick upon Tweed 7314
Potter Peter Thomas works
here with Margaret Wilson,

weaver. The pots are based
on traditional English
earthenware using local clay
and glaze materials.
Margaret Wilson
handweaves rugs with
design based on the
surrounding sea and
landscape.

Ulverston
Corn Mill Galleries
The Old Town Mill,
Ulverston, Cumbria. Tel
Ulverston 54600
Galleries show a selection of
quality jewellery, ceramics,
weaving, glass and
embroidery, and the work
of the *Wendy Todd Textile
Workshop*, which is also in
the building. These are
screen-printed fashion and
furnishing items. In
addition there is a museum
displaying the recently
restored waterwheel and
17th-c. corn-grinding
machinery.

Washington
Biddick Farm Arts Centre
Biddick Lane, Fatfield,
Washington, Tyne &
Wear. Tel Washington
466440
Four different craft
workshops are based at this
centre: pottery, wood-
turning, violin making and
experimental glass work
which includes stained glass
windows and fused glass.

York
The Castle Museum
Tower Street, York. Tel
York 53611. Apr-Sep, Mon-
Sat 9.30-6, Sun 10-4.30;
Oct-Mar, Mon-Sat 9.30-
4.30, Sun 10-4.30
Large general folk museum
with collection of artefacts.
Also craft workshops in
room settings.

John Gaastra
6 Moorlands Road, Skelton,
York. Tel York 470328
Tapestry weaver selling his
work directly to the public.
Visitors can see his work in
progress.

Tofts
10 The Shambles, York.
Tel York 56470
Shop specializing in
humorous pottery; its owner
Tim Mitchinson produces
slip-cast earthenware,
sometimes practical but
with emphasis on modelled
and moulded decoration.
Also stocks the work of
other potters and small
manufacturing companies
working in the same vein.

ISLE OF MAN

The Cregneash Folk Museum
nr Port St Mary, Isle of
Man. Mid-May-late Sep,
Mon-Sat 10-1, 2-5, Sun 2-5
Collection of cottages and
workshops illustrating the
life of a crofting and fishing
community. They include a
weaver's shed with hand
loom, a woodturner's
workshop with treadle
lathe, and a smithy.
Spinning demonstrations on
certain days and
occasionally a blacksmith
working.

St George's Woollen Mills
Laxey, Isle of Man. Tel
Laxey 395
Handwoven woollen Manx
tweeds and travelling rugs.
Local sheepskins, woven
and knitted items also
available.

Tynwald Craft Centre
Tynwald Mills, St John's,
Isle of Man. Tel St John's
213
An old woollen mill which
houses craft shops and
workshops, including
Tynwald Mills, weavers of
tweed, rugs and blankets; *St
John's Crystal*, blown glass;
Charles Alexander, jeweller
and silversmith; *The Mill
Pottery*, handthrown
earthenware.

Wales

Clwyd, Dyfed, Glamorgan, Gwent, Gwynedd and Powys

Much of Wales is a land of lush, wet pastures, hills and woods. Not surprisingly the traditional crafts reflect this. There has been a revival of both wool crafts (from the sheep) and leatherwork (from the cattle). The quantity of wood in the forests along the Welsh borders provided many with a living from woodworking: turning (including many utensils made for the local dairies), furniture making – the most traditional piece being the Welsh dresser – and carving. Carved wooden love tokens, mainly highly-decorated love spoons, were a folk tradition, which has recently been revived. Welsh slate is an excellent building material, but it can also be carved and cut with letters. Although this was traditionally the province of the monumental mason, attempts are now being made by other craftsmen to adapt slate to new decorative forms.

Wales has a strong cultural identity: Welsh people take great pride in their language and heritage. This often takes expression in the use of old Celtic patterns and forms as decoration for modern craftwork. Traditionally, the exquisite, distinctive interlacing and whorls were used on metalwork, stonecarving and illuminated manuscript. The consummate skill of this work is hard to follow, but many modern craftsmen have taken up the challenge with enthusiasm and imagination.

Aberbargoed

Stuart Crystal
Pengam Glassworks, Angel Lane, Aberbargoed, Mid Glamorgan. Tel Bargoed 831617
Makers of handmade lead crystal tableware. The blowing, processing, marking and decorating of the glass can be seen.

Anglesey

Anglesey Pottery
Pretty Cottage, Amlwch Port, Anglesey Gwynedd. Tel Amlwch 830096
James and Patricia Hutchins' pottery where they make handthrown pottery decorated with modelled birds' heads. Also dishes and plates decorated with Celtic designs. Workshop only open by arrangement.

Bangor

Llanfair ym Muallt Pottery
Penrhyn Castle, Bangor, Gwynedd
Produces pottery decorated with Celtic interlaced designs, and pottery chess sets.

Bangor-on-Dee

J. Johnson & Sons
Station Road, Bangor-on-Dee, nr Wrexham, Clwyd. Tel Wrexham 780417
Basket-makers using their own locally grown willows. Workshop only open by arrangement.

Betws-y-Coed

Betws-y-Coed Potters and Weavers
Betws-y-Coed, Gwynedd. Tel B.-y-C. 224
Produces a range of earthenware with pierced cut-out patterns, also small woven goods in pure wool. Adjoining shop also sells stoneware by other potters.

Boncath

Ty Gwydraid Studio
Ty Gwydraid Studio, Abercych, Boncath, Dyfed. Tel Boncath 421
Craftsmen in stained glass: restorations as well as new work. Workshop not open to the public.

Cardiff

Anna Adam, Weaver
Blair Athol Cottage, Lisvane Road, Llanishen, Cardiff. Tel Cardiff 759779
Using handspun and vegetable-dyed local wool, Anna Adam weaves wall-hangings, tapestries, rugs, cushions, table mats, scarves and shawls.

Things Welsh
3-7 Duke Street Arcade, Cardiff. Tel Cardiff 33445
Shop which, as its name suggests, stocks only Welsh crafts: pottery, wood, leather, slate, tapestry, jewellery, etc.

Church Stoke
Churchstoke Pottery
Old School, Church Stoke,
Powys. Tel Church Stoke
511
Owen Thorpe makes a full
range of domestic stoneware
pottery, decorated with
coloured slips and wax-
resist brushwork. Also
produces individual pieces.

Cilgerran
Snail Trail Handweavers
Penwenallt Farm,
Cilgerran, nr Cardigan,
Dyfed. Tel Boncath 228
Using local fleece from
Welsh Mountain sheep,
Martin and Nina
Weatherhead spin and
weave, producing floor
rugs, wall-hangings,
cushions and bags. From
Apr to Oct they run
residential courses and
tuition in weaving, spinning
and dyeing.

Clyro
Harold Coates
The Coach House, Clyro, nr
Hay on Wye, Powys. Tel
Hay on Wye 820814
Glass engraver and
miniature painter. Uses
diamond point stipple and
tungsten carbide point on
goblets, window panes and
panels. Much work is to
commission.

Wye Pottery
Clyro, nr Hay-on-Wye,
Powys. Tel Hay-on-Wye
820510
Adam Dworski started the
Wye pottery in 1956, where
he makes majolica using
brushwork decoration. Also
figures, plaques and pots in
oxidised stoneware and a
little porcelain.

Corris
Alison Morton
Bron-y-gan, Corris, nr
Machynlleth, Powys. Tel
Corris 629
Weaver who makes
handwoven floor rugs,
travel rugs, shawls,
cushions, tweed and rag
rugs.

Criccieth
Charles Jones, Woodcarver
Promenade, Criccieth,
Gwynedd. Tel Criccieth
2833
Welsh love spoons carved in
over 60 traditional designs.
Also corner cupboards,
stools, etc.

Crickhowell
Grahame Amey
The Granary, Standard
Street, Crickhowell, Powys.
Tel Crickhowell 810540
Furniture-making work-
shop in 13th-c. granary and
malt house. Traditional and
modern pieces mainly in
oak and ash: Welsh
dressers, refectory tables,
rocking chairs, milking
stools, etc. Associated craft
shop, *Hurdy Gurdy*, nearby.

Denbigh
Brookhouse Pottery
Brookhouse Lane,
Denbigh, Clwyd. Tel
Denbigh 2805
David and Margaret Frith
make a range of domestic
ware and individual pieces
in stoneware and porcelain.

Dinas Cross
Cemaes Pottery and Ceramics
Parc-y-Gilwen, Dinas
Cross, Dyfed. Tel Dinas
Cross 376
Leonard Rees's pottery sells
domestic ware, tiles, garden
pots, etc. Workshop not
open to the public.

Ewenny
Ewenney Pottery,
nr Bridgend, Mid
Glamorgan. Tel Bridgend
3020
Old-established family
pottery producing hand-
thrown earthenware.

Haverfordwest
*Stephen Paddon, Goldsmith
and Silversmith*
1 St Mary Street,
Haverfordwest, Dyfed. Tel
Haverfordwest 67976
Handmade gold and silver
jewellery, spoons and boxes
sold in gallery. Workshop
not open to the public.

Holywell
Holywell Textile Mills
Holywell, Clwyd. Tel
Holywell 712022
Carding, spinning and
weaving of woollen cloth,
particularly tweeds.
Knitting wool spun from
Jacob sheep in their natural
colours.

Kilgetty
Pinnocchio Leather
Carmarthen Road, Kilgetty,
Dyfed. Tel Saundersfoot
812115
David Thomas Palmer,
leather craftsman, hand
cuts, tools, dyes, stitches
and finishes handbags,
belts, wallets, etc., from
quality British hides.

Avondale Glass
Carmarthen Road, Kilgetty,
Dyfed. Tel Saundersfoot
813345
Vincenzo Speranza, glass-
maker and blower, produces
glass fruit, vases, dishes,
paperweights, birds, etc.
Studio open in mornings:
separate shop.

Llanidloes
Black Sheep Weavers
1 Great Oak Street,
Llanidloes, Powys. Tel
Llanidloes 2959
Workshop handweaving
floor rugs, cushions, wall-
hangings, lampshades and
fabric lengths in wool, some
from fleeces of Black
Welsh, Welsh Mountain
and Grey Welsh sheep.

Susan Whitehead Jewellery
Aberbidno, Llangurig,
Llanidloes, Powys. Tel
Llanidloes 647
Jewellery studio where
Susan Whitehead works in
silver and gold.

Llangefni
Bodeilio Weaving Centre
Talwrn, nr Llangefni, Isle
of Anglesey. Tel Llangefni
722465
Permanent exhibition on
history of handweaving,
both local and foreign.
Professional weavers can be
seen at work (work for sale).

Llandysul
Yr Hen Ysgol
Aberbanc, nr Llandysul,
Dyfed. Tel Velindre 370771
Workshop of Mary Lloyd
Jones, tapestry weaver and
painter (includes work on
silk and cotton) and John
Jones, rug weaver. The
small gallery shows their
work and handwoven rugs,
tapestries, handwoven and
handknitted clothes,
jewellery, woodcrafts,
ceramics and glass by other
local craftsmen. Textile
courses also run from here.

Llawhaden
Ridgeway Pottery
Llawhaden, Dyfed. Tel
Llawhaden 268
Stoneware pottery
specializing in bread crocks,
plant pots, large bowls and
teapots.

Login
Studio in the Church
Login, nr Whitland, Dyfed.
Tel Clynderwen 676
Studio of weavers Alan
Hemmings and Jane Harris,
who make handloomed
clothes and accessories in
mohair and Welsh spun
wool; each design is in a
signed limited edition. Shop
sells wools and other crafts.
Annual exhibition of handloom weaving.

Nantmor
Corlwyni Pottery
Nantmor, Caernarvon,
Gwynedd. Tel Beddgelert
331
Michael Cole's pottery
makes domestic stoneware,
such as mugs, teapots and
casseroles, and also more
decorative pieces: vases,
bowls, bottles. Workshop
open and a range of work is
on view and for sale.

Narberth
The Narberth Pottery
2 Market Street, Narberth,
Dyfed. Tel Narberth
860732
Simon Rich's pottery,
where he makes stoneware
decorated with colour glazes
and brush painting.

Newbridge-on-Wye
*Mid Wales Craft Shop and
Gallery*
Newbridge-on-Wye,
Powys. Tel Newbridge-on-
Wye 364
Gallery and craft shop
showing studio pottery,
handspun and knitted
clothes, woodwork, silver,
toys and glass.

Newcastle Emlyn
*James Davies (Abercŷch) &
Co. Ltd*
Newbridge Sawmills,
Cenarth, Newcastle Emlyn,
Dyfed. Tel Llechryd 286
Old-established family
business of wood-workers,
producing hay rakes,
milking stools, chopping
boards. Patterns and
methods of manufacture
centuries old. Items can be
bought directly from the
sawmill. Workshop not
open to the public.

Porthmadog
Porthmadog Pottery
Snowdon Mill, Snowdon
Street, Porthmadog,
Gwynedd. Tel Porthmadog
2785
Produces earthenware and
handthrown stoneware.
Also sells quality crafts by
other Welsh craftsmen.

Pwllheli
*John Davies/Gwynedd
Pottery*
Glyddyn Mawr, Y Ffor,
Pwllheli, Gwynedd. Tel
Pwllheli 2932
Functional stoneware
pottery made by traditional
methods. Many of the
glazes are made from locally
gathered materials. Write or
telephone first to visit the
workshops.

Rhandirmwyn
Towy Pottery
Rhandirmwyn, Llandovery,
Dyfed. Tel Rhandirmwyn
206
Bill Marno's pottery
workshop can only be seen
by arrangement, but he sells
a wide range of wood-fired
and gas-fired pots, mostly
domestic stoneware.

St Fagans
Welsh Folk Museum
St Fagan's, nr Cardiff. Tel
Cardiff 569441. Mon-Sat
10-5, Sun 2.30-5; closed
Christmas Day, Boxing
Day, Good Friday and New
Year's Day
Displays of traditional
Welsh crafts: wood-carving,
needlework, pottery. Also
gives demonstrations of
crafts. A number of typical
Welsh buildings have been
re-erected in the grounds.
Welsh Craft Shop sells
quality work.

Solva
The Craftsman
3 Main Street, Solva, nr
Haverfordwest, Dyfed.
Furniture maker producing
plain country pieces: rush-
seated chairs, dressers,
refectory tables, etc.

Swansea
Celtic Studios
5 Prospect Place (Somerset
Place), Swansea W.
Glamorgan. Tel Swansea
54833
Stained glass studio where
artists and craftsmen can be
seen at work.

Tregaron
*Canolfan Cynllun Crefft
Cymru (Craft Design Centre
of Wales)*
Tregaron, Dyfed. Tel
Tregaron 415
Craft shop giving emphasis
to Welsh materials,
language, country crafts and
traditions. Knitwear and
weaving from Welsh wool
can be seen.

Clocsiau Caron
Tregaron, Dyfed. Tel
Tregaron 8925
J. H. J. Davies makes clogs
by hand in traditional and
new styles. He uses local
wood; the leather uppers are
made with some help from a
saddler.

Tregaron Pottery
Castell Flemish, Tregaron,
Dyfed. Tel Bronant 639
Handthrown stoneware,
some decorated with Welsh
script and dragons.

Northern Ireland

County Antrim, County Armagh, County Down, County Fermanagh, County Londonderry and County Tyrone

Ireland has long been famous for the cultivation of flax and the manufacture of linen thread and cloth. Partly as a result of this the making of crochet lace was established in the 19th century and remains to this day, though to a much lesser extent, a craft for which the region is famed. It was in 19th-century Ireland that the beauties and possibilities of the art were fully explored and Irish crochet work became sought after throughout Europe. Some of the early work imitated *guipure* laces, but crochet lace was most frequently made into decorative edgings. Aran jerseys, originating from the fishing communities, have now been adopted as a traditional Irish pattern.

Ballygally
Ballygally Farm Pottery
3 Croft Road, Ballygally, Co Antrim. Tel Ballygally 364
Jeanette Lammey produces decorated earthenware and terracotta. Craft shop.

Belfast
James Watson Stained Glass
Unit 3, Falcon Road, Belfast. Tel Belfast 692425
Designer and manufacturer of stained glass and leaded lights; also restores old stained glass. Workshop only open by arrangement.

Ulster Folk and Transport Museum
Cultra Manor, Holywood, nr Belfast. Tel Holywood 5411. May-Sep, Mon-Sat 11-7, Sun 2-7; Oct-Apr, Mon-Sat 11-5, Sun 2-5.
Indoor and outdoor exhibits include traditional crafts.

Coleraine
Knitting Craft
4-6 Bridge Street, Coleraine, Co Londonderry. Tel Coleraine 3878
Workshop and showroom with knitwear, tapestries, wall-hangings, rugs, etc.

Donaghcloney
Beechmount Ironcraft
23 Moygannon Lane, Donaghcloney, Co Down. Tel Waringstown 881162
Blacksmith producing decorative wrought ironwork: gates, railings, garden furniture, etc., as well as repairs and welding.

Dungannon
Kenneth Black, Jeweller
139 Drumaney Road, Dungannon, Co Tyrone. Tel Coagh 573
Individually designed and made gold and silver jewellery using precious and semi-precious stones.

Dunmanagh
Mill Pottery
Brook Road, Dunmanagh, Co Tyrone. Tel Dunmanagh 377
Tom Agnew's pottery, with wide range of domestic stoneware.

Glenarm
Jewellery Workshops and Craft Gallery
Toberwine Street, Glenarm, Co Antrim. Tel Glenarm 445
Modern jewellery and silverware incorporating precious metals, titanium, stones and acrylic. Shop also sells general crafts. Workshops not open to public.

Hillsborough
P.R. Cowdy Crafts
28 Main Street, Hillsborough, Co Down. Tel Hillsborough 682455
Shop selling wide range of work from Britain and the Republic of Ireland.

Graham Harron & Co
12 Main Street, Hillsborough, Co Down. Tel Hillsborough 683102
Individually handmade jewellery and silver. Work mostly to commission.

Lisburn
CWS Design
Mill Street, Hilden, Lisburn, Co Antrim. Tel Lisburn 70364
Designers and makers of stained and decorative glass, and engravers of glass.

Newry
John McAtasney
79 Canal Street, Newry, Co Down. Tel Newry 61605
Hand-loom weaver of woollen tweeds, etc., and of linen – both plain and damask weave, from local flax. The damask loom is over 150 years old and the only one of its kind still worked in Ireland.

Rostrevor
Gerd and Karen Hay-Edie, Weavers
86 Killowen Old Road, Rostrevor, nr Newry, Co Down. Tel Rostrevor 38373
Handwoven tweed, floor rugs, wall-hangings, furnishing fabrics. Some work uses the natural fleece from the Mourne region.

Swatragh
Glenshane Cottage Industries
Main Street, Swatragh, Co Londonderry. Tel Swatragh 246/7
Produces handknitted pure wool clothes in the traditional Aran stitches.

Scottish Lowlands

Central, Borders, Dumfries & Galloway, Fife, Lothian, Strathclyde and Tayside

The Lowlands have a wide range of crafts, many of them distinctively Scottish. A rich tradition of hand loom weaving is shown in many of the most famous products: the tweeds, tartans and Paisley shawls. The wool comes from the sheep farmed along the Borders, and bracken, lichen and seaweeds for dyeing the wools are plentiful. There is also a strong tradition of high-loom tapestry work produced by various Scottish studios, most notably the Edinburgh Tapestry Studio. (Founded in 1912, this studio translates the work of many internationally known artists into tapestries.)

During the 1890s a Glasgow group, inspired by artist and architect Charles Rennie Mackintosh and working in the spirit of the Arts and Crafts Movement, produced finely-made stained glass, jewellery, metalwork, enamels and embroidery. Their work has had a profound influence on Scottish craftsmen to this day.

Aberdour
Moray Workshop
High Street, Aberdour, Fife. Tel Aberdour 860248
Maureen Wilkie, jeweller, works in silver decorated with engraving and repoussé enamelling.

Appin
Appin Pottery
Glen Creran, Appin, Oban, Strathclyde. Tel Appin 319
Joe Finch's pottery, where he makes a range of domestic and decorative wood-fired stoneware.

Bridge of Dee
John Davey
Old Bridge, Bridge of Dee, Castle Douglas, Dumfries & Galloway. Tel Bridge of Dee 239
Handbuilt ceramic sculpture and stoneware with surface decoration. Pottery not open to public.

Clachan
Fiadh Mor Antlercraft
Battery Point, Clachan, Strathclyde. Tel Clachan 226
Sells walking sticks, cutlery, buttons and jewellery made from local deer antlers.

Comrie
Comrie Crafts
Drummond Street, Comrie, Tayside. Tel Comrie 70646
Craftworkers in deer horn and wood; showroom also has a selection of other hand-made Scottish crafts.

Museum of Scottish Tartans
Comrie, Tayside. Tel Comrie 779. Apr-Nov, Mon-Sat 9-5, Sun 2-5; Nov-Mar, Mon-Fri 10-4, Sat 10-1
Collection of highland dress and Scottish tartans. Reconstructed early 18th-c. weaver's cottage. Hand spinning and vegetable dyeing demonstrations.

Crieff
Pibroch Crafts
86 Burrell Street, Crieff, Tayside. Tel Crieff 3197
Leatherworkers making soft leather pouch sporrans and handbags. Hand cutting, skiving and sewing the leather can be seen in progress.

Drymen
Drymen Pottery
The Square, Drymen, nr Glasgow. Tel Drymen 60458
Shirley Bracewell produces handthrown stoneware pottery. Adjoining shop also sells other craftwork.

Edinburgh
Canon Mills Pottery
5 Warriston Road, Edinburgh 3. Tel Edinburgh 556 5904 (before 9 or eves)
Janet Adam's studio pottery in an 18th-c. farm cottage, where she makes and sells domestic stoneware and some decorative pieces.

Glass Works
14/16 Holyrood Road, Edinburgh. Tel Edinburgh 556 2129
Three craftworkers in original glass blown free-hand are based here. Work can be seen in progress. There is also a gallery selling the work of other glassmakers, regular exhibitions of ceramics, painting and jewellery.

Nether Lennie Pottery
Cammo Road, Edinburgh. Tel. Edinburgh 334 2783
Susan Mason works in blue and white porcelain, both domestic and individual pieces. Demonstrations if work is in progress.

New Solen Gallery
Jeffrey Street, Edinburgh. Tel Edinburgh 557 3032
One floor has a permanent display and sale of work by the Scottish Craftsmen Furniture Makers Association. Also a floor of mainly Scots crafts: wood, ceramics, weaving, etc.

Stockbridge Workshop
33 Circus Lane, Edinburgh.
Tel Edinburgh 226 5497
Jewellers Margaret Fleming
and Graham Crimmins
make and sell their
jewellery.

The Scottish Craft Centre
140 Canongate, Royal Mile,
Edinburgh. Tel Edinburgh
556 8136
Centre for quality Scottish
crafts: pottery, weaving,
knitting, silver, woodwork,
glass and jewellery.
Changing exhibitions of
work by various craftsmen.

Textile Workshop and Gallery
166 High Street,
Edinburgh. Tel Edinburgh
225 4570
Workshop where weaving,
spinning, crochet,
smocking, tapestry, knitting
and dyeing are all taught.
Exhibitions throughout the
year on different aspects of
textiles and work for sale.

Falkirk
MacIntosh Glass
Unit 4, Dalderse Avenue,
Falkirk, Central. Tel
Falkirk 37986
Alastair MacInstosh makes
a range of vases and scent
bottles decorated with
spiralling threads of
coloured glass. His wine
glasses are decorated with
air twist stems in the 18th-c.
manner. Workshop open by
appointment.

Galashiels
Lindean Mill Glass
Lindean Mill, Galashiels,
Borders. Tel Galashiels
20173
Handmade glass by David
Kaplan and Annica
Sandstrom. Workshop open
by appointment.

Gatehouse of Fleet
Bridget Drakeford, Potter
The Drill Hall, Castramont
Road, Gatehouse of Fleet,
Dumfries & Galloway. Tel
Gatehouse 695
Working in porcelain
making bowls and vases,
mirrors and decorative
pieces. Demonstrations of
techniques.

Glasgow
Hallibees Design
55-61 Ruthven Lane,
Glasgow G12. Tel Glasgow
339 0837
Sells jewellery, designer
knitwear, handblown and
stained glass, and other
craftwork.

Glenrothes
Balbirnie Craft Centre
by Markinch, Glenrothes,
Fife. Tel Glenrothes 755975
Eight workshops and
showroom in fine 18th-c.
coach house. Crafts include:
stoneware, domestic pottery
and sculpture, fashion,
jewellery, knitwear,
leatherworker, modern and
traditional furniture,
stained glass.

Haddington
*James Mitchell, Lammermoor
Woollens*
Mitchell's Close, Market
Street, Haddington, East
Lothian. Tel Haddington
2207
Handwoven tweeds for
ladies.

Margery Clinton Ceramics
The Pottery, Newton Port,
Haddington, East Lothian.
Tel Haddington 3584
With several assistants,
Margery Clinton produces a
range of slip-cast pieces and
tiles. She specializes in
lustre glazes, a development
of those perfected by 10th-
c. Islamic potters. Some
tiles are reproductions of
early Islamic patterns.
Workshop open Sat
mornings or by
arrangement.

Innerleithen
Quair Woodware
Traquair House,
Innerleithen, Borders. Tel
Innerleithen 830833
John Schofield and Jamie
Blair produce turned wood
items from local hardwoods:
sycamore, beech, ash, oak,
cherry walnut and yew.
Shop sells bowls, rattles,
rolling pins, porridge
spurtles and traditional
butter prints. Workshop
open Easter-end Sep.

Isle of Arran
*Silverbirch Spinning and
Weaving Workshop*
Whiting Bay, Isle of Arran,
Strathclyde
Lyn Ross spins and weaves
natural-dyed yarns.
Handspins yarns for
knitting also. From May-
Oct courses are run in
spinning, weaving and
dyeing.

Isle of Mull
Isle of Mull Silver
Ledmore, Aros, Isle of
Mull, Strathclyde. Tel Aros
378
P and B Campbell are
jewellers and silversmiths.
They make silver spoons
and quaichs in traditional
Scottish forms as well as
other small pieces.

Kelso
The Kelso Pottery
The Knowes, Kelso,
Borders. Tel Kelso 24027
Produces domestic
stoneware decorated with
coloured slips which echo
the landscape of the Border
country.

Kilbarchan
*Anne Clare Graham,
Jeweller and Silversmith*
41 High Barholm,
Kilbarchan, Strathclyde.
Tel Kilbarchan 4814
Individually made and
designed silver and gold
jewellery and small boxes,
sometimes work also
incorporates tortoiseshell,
titanium, ivory, perspex,
resins and precious stones.
If requested demonstrations
can be given.

Weaver's Cottage
Kilbarchan, Strathclyde.
May, Sep, Oct, Thur, Sat,
Sun 2-5; Jun, Jul, Aug,
daily 2-5
The National Trust for
Scotland own this 18th-c.
craftsman's house with
traditional weaving
equipment on show.

Lochgilphead
Blackthorn Workshop
Monydrain House,
Lochgilphead, Strathclyde.
Tel Lochgilphead 2884
Workshop specializing
mostly in weaving local
fleece dyed with vegetable
dyes from plants gathered
from surrounding
countryside. Produces rugs,
bags, wall-hangings, etc.,
also wooden toys, silver
jewellery and spoons.

Palnackie
North Glen Gallery
Palnackie, nr Castle
Douglas, Dumfries &
Galloway. Tel Palnackie 200
Edward Iglehart,
glassworker, has a
workshop and gallery here
where he makes blown glass
vases, bottles, bowls and
decorative pieces, both clear
and coloured, often
featuring mushrooms and
fungi as a decorative theme.

Perth
The Little Gallery
90 Canal Street, Perth,
Tayside
Sells quality British crafts:
pottery, jewellery, glass,
prints, etc.

Perth Craft Centre
38 South Street, Perth,
Tayside. Tel Perth 38232
Craftsmen working here
include Kathleen Thomson,
jeweller and silversmith.
Works mainly in silver and
titanium producing
jewellery and small boxes.
John Yellowlees,
leatherworker, specializes in
hand stitching and quality
finishes of kilt belts,
sporrans, bags, holdalls etc.

Walkerburn
*Scottish Museum of Woollen
Textiles*
Tweedvale Mill,
Walkerburn, Borders. Tel
Walkerburn 281/3 Daily,
Easter-Oct.
Museum of the history of
the woollen industry in
Scotland. Weaver's shed
and tools. Demonstrations
of spinning.

Scottish Highlands and Islands

*Grampian, Highland, Western Isles,
Orkneys and Shetland Islands*

This region includes some of the most
inaccessible parts of Britain, and there is a
strong tradition of crafts based on local raw
materials. All the wool crafts – spinning,
dyeing, weaving and knitting – are practised
and have a high reputation. The sheep of the
Western Isles and Hebrides have always been
renowned for the quality of their fleece. Tweed
from the island of Harris is only one of its
famous products. Antler horn, and the rich
variety of stones (including agates, bloodstone,
marble and granite) are materials with qualities
which have attracted local craftsmen.

Scottish craftsmen are eager to use essentially
Scottish forms. One example is the *quaigh* or
quaich, a shallow circular drinking bowl with
two flat handles on either side of the rim.
These were used in the 17th and 18th centuries
and were made of silver or pewter, but are now
also made in pottery and wood.

It was Queen Victoria's enthusiasm for
Scotland which started the craze for the self-
conscious adoption of everything Scottish,
from Highland dress and tartans to dirks and
targes. This has been thoroughly exploited ever
since by the tourist trade. The Scottish
craftsmen will give you a different view of the
essence of Scotland.

Balnakeil
Far North Pottery
Balnakeil, Durness, by
Lairg, Highland. Tel
Durness 354
Handmade domestic
stoneware, also sculpture
and individual pieces.

Barrock
Barrock Knitwear
Ivy Cottage, Barrock,
Highland. Tel. Barrock
353.
Individually made knitwear
including traditional Fair
Isle and Shetland designs.

Bonar Bridge
*Kyleside Weaving and
Handcraft*
Bonar Bridge, Highland.
Tel Ardgay 269
Sells tweed and other woven
goods, and horn buttons
made from stag's antlers.

Braemar
The Woodcraft Shop
Invercauld Road, Braemar,
Grampian
Wood turning and carving
workshop showing all the
processes from raw material
to finished pieces.

93

Brough
Allen Whitehead,
Leatherworker
Candleberry Cottage,
Brough, Highland. Tel
Barrock 333
Works in fine heavy
cowhide; dying, stitching
and tooling the leather by
hand.

Michael O'Donnell,
Woodturner
The Croft, Brough,
Highland. Tel Barrock 605
Specializes in bowls made
from Scottish hardwoods
such as tulipwood, holly,
etc.

Drinisheader
Croft Crafts Harris
Plochropool, Drinisheader,
Harris, Highland.
Designing and weaving of
Harris tweed and plying of
Harris tweed yarn into knitting
wool. Knitwear also sold.

Eriskay
Co Chomunn Eirisgeidh
Community Hall, Eriskay,
South Uist, Outer
Hebrides. Tel Eriskay 236
Sells traditional handknitted
fisherman's jerseys which
are seamless (being knitted
on four needles).

Fort William
Scottish Crafts Exhibition
135–9 High Street, Fort
William, Highland. Tel
Fort William 2504
Gallery selling all types of
crafts made in Scotland.

Gollanfield
Culloden Pottery
The Old Smiddy,
Gollanfield, Highland. Tel
Ardersier 2340
Pottery producing
handthrown stoneware,
earthenware and procelain.
Also craft shop.

Isle of Skye
Eva Lambert
Carnach, Waternish, Isle of
Skye, Highland. Tel
Waternish 297
Weaver of tapestries, rugs,
carpets, floor pillows etc.,
using handspun fleeces
dyed with local plants.

Richard Townsend
The Workshop, 9
Peinchorran, The Braes, nr
Portree, Isle of Skye,
Highland. Tel Sligachan
226
Furniture maker and
wood turner, work can be
seen in progress.

Struan Craft Workshop
Struan, Isle of Skye,
Highland. Tel Struan 284
Kathleen Lindsley prints
wood engravings and relief
prints on a mid 19th-c.
Albion hand press. Enamel
jewellery, Harris tweed, and
local handspun, vegetable-
dyed knitwear also on show.

Kingussie
The Highland Folk Museum
Kingussie, Highland. Tel
Kingussie 307. Apr-Oct,
Mon-Sat 10-6, Sun 2-6;
Nov-to Mar, Mon-Sat 10-3
Museum includes examples
of traditional Highland
crafts and craft tools, also
extensive farming museum.

Laggan Bridge
Caoldair Pottery
Laggan Bridge, Highland
Hand made wood-fired
domestic and docorative
stoneware made by Mick
Arnold and Linda Whitty.

Lyth
Lyth Arts Centre
Lyth, nr Wick, Highland.
Tel Lyth 270. Jun 26-Sep 6
Local craftsmen: weaving,
turned wood, pottery and
embroidered textiles.

Monymusk
Bill Brown
Monyroad, Monymusk, nr
Inverurie, Grampian. Tel
Monymusk 375
Potter working in porcelain
and stoneware.

Orkney
Robert H. Towers
Rosegarth, St Ola,
Kirkwall. Tel Kirkwall
3521
Chair-maker in the style
traditional to the Orkneys;
the frames of pine and the
backs of local straw.

Tankerness House Museum
Broad Street, Kirkwall. Tel
Kirkwall 3218. Mon-Sat
10.30-1, 2-5.
Examples of the crafts of the
area, as well as folklore and
archaeology.

The Workshop
Back Road, St Margaret's
Hope, Orkney. Tel St
Margaret's Hope 201
Co-operative selling local
crafts: knitting in Icelandic
patterns, Shetland wool
jerseys in Fair Isle patterns,
handthrown pottery, etc.
Pottery open to visitors.

Strathdon
Strathdon Pottery
Strathdon, Grampian. Tel
Strathdon 241
Zelda Mowat is the only
potter in Scotland making
salt-glazed stoneware. Also
kitchenware, ovenware and
tableware. Pottery open by
appointment.

Talmine
Achnahuaigh Hand
Embroideries
Talmine, nr Tongue,
Highland. Tel Talmine 277
Shop selling work of Maggi
Thomason: fine embroidery
applied to pictures, clothes
and samplers, as well as
traditional smocking. Also
the work of other
embroiderers.

Thurso
Fisherbiggin Pottery Studio
Millers Terrace, Riverside,
Thurso, Highland. Tel
Thurso 3318
Potters Mary and Fred
Barclay produce a wide
range of domestic and
decorative handthrown
stoneware using peat-ash
glazes.

Tongue
M. Sutherland, Weaver
Woodend, Tongue,
Highland. Tel Tongue 235
Mr Sutherland can be seen
handweaving tweeds and
tartan each day. Showroom
stocked with handknitted
Fair Isle, turned wood and
leather work.

Index